Anxiety is an Illusion

The Proven 3-Week Plan to Overcome Worry, Fear, and Panic Attacks

by

Prof. Dr. Detlef Beeker

www.detlefbeeker.de/en

Prof. Dr. Detlef Beeker
Happiness Researcher

Disclaimer

including international, federal, state, and local governing professional licensing, business practices, advertising, and all other aspects of doing business in the US, Canada, or any other jurisdiction is the sole responsibility of the purchaser or reader.

Neither the author nor the publisher assumes any responsibility or liability whatsoever on the behalf of the purchaser or reader of these materials. Any perceived slight of any individual or organization is purely unintentional.

Contents

Free Gift

"The clearest sign of wisdom is a consistently good mood." — Michel de Montaigne

Do you remember the first time you fell in love? Everything was suddenly wonderful: The sky never looked bluer and more beautiful, nor its puffy, white clouds prettier. Even the rain was enjoyable!

Now, what if you could have this lovely mood *all* the time? In my book, *18 Surprising Good-Mood Tips*, available in the link below, I will show you how to do just that.

http://detlefbeeker.de/en/gift/

Don't let its small size fool you: At 52 pages, *18 Surprising Good-Mood Tips* packs tons of information, tips, and guidance that, if implemented, will change your life. Here's just a snippet of what you'll be able to experience through this free resource:

- Improve your mood and health by pressing specific body parts that I'll teach you.
- Use proven mental tactics to get into a good mood in seconds.
- Quickly increase your good mood using secret yoga techniques.
- Discover this unknown piece of music that is scientifically proven to be the best stress reducer ever.
- Learn relaxation and self-confidence from James Bond himself.
- Be able to relax in 10 seconds.
- Practice this mind-boggling technique that makes you more refreshed and revitalized.
- Find and use the best apps to relieve your stress and give you relaxation and serenity.
- Discover the Fidget Cube and how it works.
- Gain a new generation of good-mood techniques.
- And much, much more!

This book gives you access to the results of my twenty-year career as a happiness researcher. It's given me not just the honor and joy, but the *ability* to spread wellbeing around the world—I'm thrilled I get to do it once again!

To thank you for your investment in time and energy in

Anxiety is an Illusion, I'd like to offer you *18 Surprising Good-Mood Tips*, completely free of charge. I'm delighted that you said 'YES!' to the adventure of meditation done right and privileged to guide you through it. All you have to do to access your gift is click the simple link below.

http://detlefbeeker.de/gift/

About the Author

"The universe is friendly."

International Amazon best-selling author Prof. Dr. Detlef Beeker is a happiness researcher and an anti-stress expert. He has been researching these fields for more than twenty years and has written numerous books touching on various topics in this wide field.

But Detlef is not just an author. He is a man who practices what he preaches. He has been meditating for more than twenty years. Which is perhaps what makes him down-to-earth in his approach to teaching. Too many self-help guides give you big ideas but fail to show you how to make their teaching applicable to your life. In his books, Detlef Beeker offers practical methods and step-by-step instructions that can be implemented immediately.

At the age of seven, Dr. Beeker had already found his destiny. "I want to become a taster in a pudding factory," he told his mum. Although his vocation has changed since then, his deep desire to make the world a sweeter place is as intact today as it was back then.

Visit his website http://detlefbeeker.de/en to find stacks of helpful tips, tricks, and a gift for you!

Chapter 1: Anxiety makes us heroes

"In every adversity lies an equal or greater benefit."
— Napoleon Hill

It just has to be said: Life can be quite annoying. It is full of adversities and problems: diseases, stress, fears, pain, loss of job, dentist, cockroaches and Rolfing (apologies to my nice Rolfing therapist). Why are there all these annoying hassles? Because they make us stronger. It's like lifting weights - it's damned exhausting, but your muscles develop and you get stronger. Do you know the movie Matrix? The main actor is Neo. His archrival is Agent Smith. He follows Neo and makes his life difficult. Neo has to get better and stronger so that he can fight Agent Smith. Finally, Neo attains enlightenment and defeats Smith.

Would Neo have become enlightened if it hadn't been for Smith? No! It was only because of Agent Smith that Neo became so strong.

Agent Smith turned Neo into a hero. Just as Agent Smith challenges Neo, our fear forces us to leave our comfort zone. It forces us to become wise and courageous. In short, our fear turns us into heroes. By the way, you are not alone. Fear is a widespread disease. More than 16.5 million people in the USA suffer from panic attacks.

I used to suffer from panic attacks myself - for years, sometimes suffering several attacks a day. It was terrible. For me, that period of my life was the dark night of the soul. But there is no better motivation than panic attacks. It was the beginning of my path: I really wanted to learn how to fight off panic attacks and as quickly as possible. Since then, I have read hundreds of books, attended numerous workshops, participated in countless retreats and engaged in spirituality. I have even oriented my profession accordingly. Would I have become a happiness scientist if I hadn't been a sufferer of panic attacks many years ago? Probably not!

"Only a rough sea makes a good sailor."

When all is said and done, it was those panic attacks that have steered my life in wonderful directions. They have made me stronger and wiser. On particularly insightful days, I am even grateful to my fears for supporting me so much.

I have learned great and efficient techniques to overcome fears. I developed some techniques, like BELL or APB, myself to have even better tools for warding off anxiety. You will find the best of these methods in this book.

1.1 Why this book is different

You've probably already read a lot of books, tried techniques and approaches to overcome your anxieties. You may have even attended workshops and done therapies. None of them really worked for you, right? How do I know? Because if they had, you wouldn't be reading this book. What can this book offer you what others haven't? How can this book offer you real and practical help to overcome your anxiety? Let me give you a comparison:

My friend Felix went to see a doctor the other day. Felix had something wrong with his stomach. His doctor was a general practitioner with his main emphasis on naturopathy. He gave Felix a prescription for an anti-acid, a herbal remedy and a homeopathic remedy. In addition, the doctor put an acupuncture needle in Felix's ear. Felix was supposed to leave it there for a week. The doctor used all kinds of different methods, orthodox medicine (allopathy), phytotherapy, homeopathy, and even Chinese medicine. Most importantly, what the doctor prescribed helped.

This is the way physical ailments are treated nowadays - but usually not psychological ailments. If you read a guide on cognitive behavioral therapy, you will only be offered cognitive techniques. If you browse through an energy psychology guide, only energy methods will be dealt with.

This book is all about freeing you from your anxiety. I don't care what school the techniques come from. The only important thing is that the techniques work! I have taken the best methods from a range of approaches. So, we are addressing your fears with not just one approach but with a number of approaches.

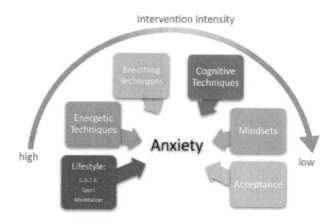

Anxiety is a complex phenomenon. If it had been easy to combat, you would have succeeded long ago. So there clearly have to be several approaches. In the graph above, you can see different categories of techniques, like breathing techniques, energetic techniques and so on. These technique categories are arranged according to the impact of the intervention. For example, a breathing technique has a greater impact than acceptance. In the following chapters, you will find out exactly what these various techniques consist of. This book is like a buffet of the most effective techniques, regardless of the school they originate from. In this book, you will find only cherry-picked methods - tried and tested - and, effective!

In this book, you will discover...

- Three 3-week programs that help you to quickly get to grips with worries, anxieties, and panic attacks.
- Anti-Panic Breathing, a special, extremely powerful breathing technique that helps you get panic attacks under control.
- Eutaptics: the fastest and most effective technique in energy psychology.
- How to resolve stress, worry, and anxiety in seconds with a scientifically proven technique.
- How C.A.T.S. can help you eliminate your fears and panic without having to use a technique.
- Simple methods that permanently calm your stressed nervous system.
- Three powerful mindsets that put you in a powerful mental state.
- 3 surprising methods of integrating mindsets into your life. You will start to see the world in a new light.
- The Work Plus: Byron Katie's fantastic method The Work extended by one element to fight fear even better.
- 4-Minute Chi Boost gives your energy a boost in just a few minutes. It works in the case of fears, panic attacks, and many diseases.
- BELL: The fastest relaxation technique.
- The new generation of thought-stopping techniques. These techniques are guaranteed to

immediately stop your negative thoughts.
- How the revolutionary Sedona method helps you let go of your negative emotions in seconds. This technique has been proven hundreds of thousands of times.
- ... and much more.

1.2 How anxiety is created: A cockroach under a bathmat

In order to combat anxiety, we must first look at how it arises. Here's a story about this:

For a few years now, I've enjoyed going on holiday in Asia. Thailand, in particular, has been a real hit with me. Beautiful beaches, relaxed people, delicious food. There is only one thing in Thailand that rocks my boat: cockroaches! They are huge there, in some cases the size of a thumb. Just between you and me: I'm afraid of these Godzilla cockroaches. My wife thinks it's funny: "You're much taller than the cockroaches. Why are you afraid? She looks up at me, gently boxes me in the stomach and grins. She is small, a mere 1.52 m, long black hair, sparkling eyes. She is also as fast as Bruce Lee. Cockroaches have no chance against her.

I can still well remember a vacation in Thailand. It was on the island Koh Samui. It was already late and my wife excitedly said to me: "I've just killed a cockroach! It's under the bathmat now." - Is it really dead? These guys are tough," I replied hysterically. In the following days, I tensed up each time I went into the bathroom. Just the thought that there was a cockroach under the bathmat

was enough to get me down. Later, my wife told me
that she had already disposed of the cockroach.

Anxieties are like non-existent cockroaches under a bathmat. Anxiety stems from the *idea* that something bad is going to happen in the future: "I will definitely die of cancer". In fact, there is no real threat at all. The fear only happens in our heads. The cockroach under the bathmat only existed in my imagination. It wasn't *really* there. Think about how many of the anxieties that *you* had, actually materialized. None at all, right?

"99% of the worries and fears will
never happen."

By the way, I was later able to overcome my fear of cockroaches. BELL and Eutaptics played an important role in this.

So, anxiety is not triggered by actual events, but by our thoughts about them. Already 2000 years ago, the former slave and great philosopher Epictetus realized:

"It is not the things themselves that
trouble us, but our ideas and opin-
ions of them."

The main cause of our fears is fearful thoughts. Besides thoughts, there are other factors that influence fears:

- **Lifestyle and nervous system**: Anxious people often have an easily excitable nervous system, i.e.

stress has a stronger effect on them than it does on people who have a balanced nervous system. So, if we suffer from anxiety, it is important that we balance our nervous system. Anxiety, worry, and panic strain our nervous system. That is why it is wise to calm it down. It's like a holiday. This is where our general way of life comes into play. There are some effective ways to strengthen your nervous system.

- **Energy system**: Acupuncture has long been recognized by the scientific world. Acupuncture has even been tried and tested by the statutory health insurance companies. It is based on the fact that diseases are caused by disturbances in the energy system. The body has energy channels, and when the energy flow is disturbed, mental and physical illnesses arise. Fear, for example, is associated with the flow of kidney energy. I.e., here we have another resource to fight our fear. In this book, we use all effective possibilities.

1.3 How to get the most out of this book

The book is structured as follows:

The ingredients: The chapter "The best techniques against worry, anxiety, and panic" contains highly effective techniques against anxiety. This is a toolbox of cherry-picked, tried and tested methods that will put an end to your worries, anxieties and panic attacks. It's like baking a cake: In this chapter, you will learn the best ingredients.

The recipe: In the chapter "3-week programs" you will find three 3-week programs, each for tackling worries, fears, and panic attacks. In these programs, the techniques described above are put together so that they work best against fears. This chapter gives you the recipe for combining the "ingredients" from the previous chapter.

The shortcut: As a bonus, I will introduce you to the best herbal remedies. You will know some of them, like Valerian. Others, like Ashwagandha, are largely unknown, but very effective. Herbal remedies will make you get there even faster, they're a shortcut, so to speak.

The final chapter is a summary of the book's most important statements.

There are three ways of working with this book:

- You can simply read the book from front to back. That way, you don't lose any information.
- If you are in a hurry, then look up the program that is right for you. The techniques described there can be found in the chapter of the book entitled technique. You familiarize yourself with the techniques and apply them according to the program. That's it!
- You can proceed intuitively. Read the techniques and *feel* what appeals to you. Experiment with these techniques. Maybe the technique "delete key" works especially well for you. In that case, apply it! It is always good to listen to your intuition, your inner coach. If you are in tune with

him, he will tell you the techniques that are especially effective for you. The only problem here is that people who suffer from fears often have far too many thoughts and are often not yet able to tune in to their intuition.

If in doubt, follow the programs. They are tried and tested and very effective. Good luck with them!

1.4 The 10% rule and the high-impact approach

Studies have shown that only 10% of all readers read more than the first chapter of a non-fiction book. Why is this so? An important reason is that these books are very thick. An average non-fiction book has at least 300 pages. This can put the reader off. The information could be presented in a much shorter form. This does not apply to all books, but a lot of books are too wordy. Too many stories and stories that are too long are told and the information that is actually important is not pinpointed, but "hidden away" in a long, ongoing text. That makes it difficult for the reader to glean the information.

"Paper is patient. Some authors
shamelessly exploit that."
– Wolfgang Mocker

It's like having a giant loaf of white bread, with a diameter of about a meter. There is a raisin in the middle of this gigantic loaf of bread. You have to first fight your way through the layers of bread until you can finally eat that one raisin. This book, by contrast, is like a small, handy roll with several raisins. With every bite, you get at least one of the delicious raisins.

Since I want to make your reading experience as enjoyable as possible, I have **made the design of** this book **user-friendly**:

- Everything is to the point: I have cut down on personal anecdotes as well as on everything that artificially inflates the content. That said, there *are* numerous case studies that are necessary to illustrate the material.
- **Language**: In my scientific career, I had to read a lot of texts that were unnecessarily incomprehensible. The authors filled their explanations with unnecessary borrowed words, abstract nouns and passive constructions embedded in long multi-clause sentences. An arbitrarily chosen example of this:

  "The result is a development of knowledge that goes into breadth and depth, which ideally keeps an eye on the historicity of the objects and their conceptions, i.e. the history of the subject itself, and a progress of knowledge related to narrow innovation zones, which has also sharply outlined the not yet known as a task."

  What's that all about? It's like when you buy a sweater but the manufacturer has knotted your sleeves. Why can't the author just express it? (If you want to know what the author actually wanted to say, see the footnote.[1])

"If you can't just explain it, you haven't understood it well enough."
– Albert Einstein

That's why I use language in this book that is as easy to understand as possible, because the subject of "anxiety" is already difficult enough.

- **Enumerations:** You will find a lot of enumerations in this book. Everything is easily accessible instead of being hidden in long texts that go on and on.
- **Introductory overviews, summaries and other hints that make your life easier:** Do you know this situation? You are in a foreign city and you are looking for a train station. You are following the street signs, but at one turn, there is one missing. You don't find the station. This book is like a very friendly city: there are signs everywhere, everyone knows where they are and where they have to go.
- **Structuring:** The book is very structured with lots of subchapters so that important information can be quickly accessed.

---

[1] To put it simply: "Each subject is different. There is less discussion in the natural sciences, more in the humanities and social sciences. That's why the texts in the various subjects sound different."

The well-known author Akash Karia called this the *high-impact approach* because the information density in this book is very high and at the same time all the information is quickly accessible. I like books like these, don't you? Books where you don't have to search for ages, where you don't have to dig deep. No way, let me hand you the golden nuggets on a silver platter.

There are a lot of great **techniques** in this book that will all help you get rid of your anxieties. The techniques are specially marked with a grey bar like this

at the beginning and end of each technique, so you can't miss them.

1.5 In a nutshell

- Anxiety can be very annoying. It is a challenge. There is always a benefit in every adversity. Anxiety forces us to become wiser and more courageous. It turns us into heroes.
- The new thing about this book is that it uses all the techniques that work. It doesn't matter what "school" they come from: cognitive techniques are mixed with energy techniques.
- In this book, I have collected the most effective techniques for fighting anxiety, such as Anti-Panic Breathing, Sedona, BELL, to name just a few.
- In many anxiety guidebooks, the general lifestyle

is overlooked. A general lifestyle is extremely important when it comes to relieving anxiety.

- You can read this book in a classic way, from front to back or (if you are in a hurry) go to the appropriate program first and then familiarize yourself with the appropriate techniques.

Chapter 2: The best techniques for warding off worry, anxiety, and panic

"The universe is friendly." – Byron Katie

What you can look forward to in this chapter:

- The 16 best techniques and systems to counter worries, anxieties, and panic attacks
- The three best mindsets to counter anxiety
- The three factors in your life that cause anxiety
- The three best ways to stop anxious thoughts
- Three fast as lightning techniques to combat anxiety
- Two methods for fighting fear on an energy level

This chapter is a toolbox containing the best techniques for beating worry, anxiety and panic. I have selected the best tools and put them together in this chapter. They are powerful techniques for beating your anxieties. Worries, anxieties, and panic are complex phenomena that often dog us for many years. Therefore, it is often not easy to let them go. The techniques in this book work on different levels and target fear from many sides so that it has no chance.

In this chapter, the techniques are introduced and, in the chapter, "3-week programs" you will learn exactly how to use the technique in question. It is like making lasagne: In this chapter, you get the best ingredients and in the next chapter you get the recipe.

2.1 The unknown means of attaining inner peace

This chapter is about *acceptance*. This is one of the many techniques for dealing with angst. Acceptance, however, has a special position. Why? You will find out a bit further below.

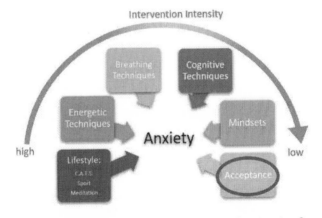

Where is the journey going? What is the destination? Most people just want inner peace. We achieve this by completely letting go of our fears.

However, there is another, unknown way of attaining inner peace: Acceptance. We simply accept that there is anxiety. Then the counterintuitive situation arises that angst and inner peace are there at the same time. That is why acceptance plays such a special role. Acceptance is the opposite of resistance. Normally, we react to unpleasant feelings with resistance, we want them to go away. Paradoxically, this leads to anxieties staying longer. If we accept them, they will go away quickly. Accepting anxieties means that we do not resist them, but give them space. They can stay there like guests in our house. So why don't we just accept all anxieties? Because they are so unpleasant. It is difficult. I recommend alleviating them first, especially in the case of strong *angst* or panic. Then, step by step, we can dare to accept them.

> *"The more we are able to accept intense negative feelings, the more peace we will have."*

Acceptance is practiced in many modern psychotherapies and spiritual systems. One of the most successful therapies "Acceptance and Commitment Therapy (ACT) even has "acceptance" in its name. By the way, "acceptance" refers to the inner experience. If we accept something, it does not automatically mean that we give up on the outside.

Ben had a colleague, Jack, who was after him. Every time he could, he would make Ben look bad in front of the boss. Ben was in his early 40s, tall and good-natured. He loved to laugh at his own jokes. Jack's behavior bothered him a lot. Ben addressed this problem in a The Work group he regularly visited (you will get to know The Work in the chapter "Warning: Your thoughts may be dangerous"). "You have no power over other people", Ursula just said: "Accept it and make peace with it". In fact, Ben managed to be at peace with it: "He's already making my working life difficult for me, so he shouldn't rob me of my inner peace," Ben thought wisely. Nevertheless, Ben took action against Jack and accused him of bullying. He was successful and Jack even received a warning. Accepting doesn't mean re-signing yourself to your fate.

How do we accept a negative feeling? The trick is that we don't listen to our thoughts but, instead, pay attention to our body sensations. Why are we doing this? I need to give you a little explanation. An emotion consists of two building blocks:

- The triggering and accompanying negative thoughts.
- The corresponding body sensations.

Let's look at an example:

Lara is worried about her child. Her child has a slight fever and cough. The talkative voice in her head whispers to her: "The fever will rise! She'll get pneumonia. Watch out!" With such negative thoughts, it's no wonder Lara's worries are getting worse. She feels the worry as a weak feeling in her stomach, a restless sensation in the middle of her body, and sweaty palms.

This example is a good illustration of how negative

emotions work. Negative thoughts trigger correspond-ing body sensations. These together make up the emo-tion. Lara has a weak feeling in her stomach etc. The negative thoughts go on and on, and as long as we lis-ten to them, we get sucked into the story. That's why it's good to pay attention to our body sensations. Even if these are supposedly negative, they are simply body sensations. Our body is always in the here and now. Our thoughts are always somewhere else. Paying attention to our body grounds us and takes us away from the neg-ative story that we are telling ourselves.

We don't just pay attention to our body sensations; no, we go one step further. We give them space. With slight feelings, this is usually not difficult. A restlessness oc-curs, we give the feeling space, and that's it. Emotions that we give a lot of space to, quickly disappear. If we fight them, however, they stay. The problem: our natu-ral reaction is to fight the unpleasant. Acceptance or ex-pansion is therefore something counter-intuitive. The more unpleasant the feeling, the harder it is for us to accept it. A slight restlessness is still O.K., but we defi-nitely want to get rid of full-grown panic. That's why I recommend other techniques for more intense feelings.

Expansion

Goal: make peace with unpleasant feelings

Technique:

1. Observe your physical sensations without judgment. If an unpleasant feeling, such as fear, arises, direct your attention to the physical sensations that come with fear. Be as curious as a scientist. Examine your body sensations. Does your body feel warm or cool? Where exactly does the body sensation occur? What color is it? Play around with it. It is important that you focus your attention on your body and not on your thoughts.

2. Breathe slowly and consciously into and around the feeling. As if you wanted to give it more space. Slow, deep, abdominal breathing is always calming. It may not make your feeling disappear, but it is a peaceful anchor in the eye of the storm.

3. Allow the feeling to be there. Give it space. Focus your attention on the physical sensations. That feeling may be unpleasant, but you let it be there. You're not fighting that feeling. You accept it. This can take a few seconds or a few minutes. Your goal is not to get rid of the feeling but to make your peace with it.

How long? How often? You can do this exercise every time unpleasant feelings arise.

Tips & Tricks:

- **Fighting is useless**. Nobody wants to have unpleasant feelings. We want to get away

29

from them as soon as possible.
Unfortunately, that doesn't work. The more we fight feelings like fear or anger, the stronger they become. That's why the only way to deal with them is to make peace with them.

- **The key is to let your feelings be there**. The aim of this exercise is not to fight and destroy unpleasant emotions but to let them be there. By making peace with them, they disappear on their own.
- **Thief in the empty house**. There is a Buddhist metaphor: the negative feeling is like a thief in an empty house. The thief comes into the house and we don't stop him. We just let him be there. The thief sees that there is nothing valuable in this house and just leaves.

Let's see how Lara uses this exercise. Her child is sick, and she is worried.

1. Observe: Lara's thoughts are going around in circles. She focuses her attention on the corresponding body sensations: Lara feels pressure and vibrations in the solar plexus. She tries to concentrate on it. She asks herself where the body sensation is occurring. This strengthens her concentration.

2. Breathe: Lara breathes deeply into the body sensation. That calms her down. The worried thoughts diminish. Also, the body sensations of worry lessen.

3. Allow: Lara allows the feeling to be there — she gives
it space. Her resistance to the unpleasant body sensations decreases. The sensations become softer and
weaker. After a while, her worries are gone.

You are welcome to use this technique for worries and
mild to moderate anxiety. Try it out.

Call to Action

Try the exercise right now. Induce an unpleasant feeling: worry, anger, inexcusability or the like. Put yourself
in a situation that annoys or frustrates you and practice
acceptance. Important: Take a slightly uncomfortable
feeling at the beginning. If you like, you can still increase
the intensity later.

2.2 Powerful mindsets

*"Even in the strifes of life, we find great gifts." – The
Bhagavad Gita*

What you can look forward to in this chapter:

- The growth mindset
- "The universe is friendly" mindset
- The "everything is fleeting" mindset
- Three methods for bringing mindsets into your
  life: Power-Person, Affirmations, Three Examples

In this chapter, we take a closer look at mindsets as a

great way to overcome fears.

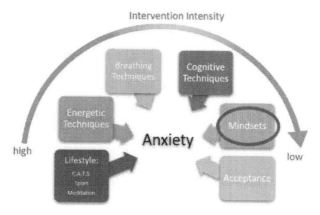

Life is full of adversities. Something that we don't want and haven't planned happens all the time: We get ill, we suffer from panic, a relative dies, we lose our job, our partner leaves us, etc. How do we deal with such adversities? Our mindset, that is, our attitude, is decisive. If we lose our job, we can moan. We can complain about how unfair this is. We can be afraid that we won't get another job. Approaching problems in this way does not help. Whining does not make the problem better. Nor does being afraid of the future.

The last section deals with the subject of "acceptance". A strong mindset promotes acceptance. The stronger our mindset, the sooner we can accept something unpleasant and be at peace with it. Mindsets are the basis. They are a powerful tool for fighting every adversity of life, including fears.

The basic attitude of every mindset is to see adversity as a challenge rather than a threat. This may seem a small difference, but it has a big effect. This attitude gives us strength and courage. A positive mindset not only improves our emotional state, it even strengthens our bodies:

A well-known study examined mothers who had a special needs child and who were the child's carer. This is an extremely high-stress situation because being a special needs child's carer is 24/7. The carer's nervous system never gets the chance to fully recuperate. The mothers were subliminally constantly on the alert. In addition, this stress was chronic, i.e. it continued over many years. On average, these mothers showed considerably more physical damage due to stress than mothers in the control group. The control group consisted of mothers with children who were not in need of care. It was also found that the longer the stress persisted, the more the body was affected. [1]

But there was one amazing peculiarity: not all carer parents showed these negative effects. There were some carer parents who could handle this stress much better, both mentally and physically. This was investigated further. In another study, the carer parents were put in a stress situation: they were supposed to solve arithmetical problems in front of an audience of doctors and professors and to give a spontaneous lecture. Such social

---

[1] Epel, E. S., et al., »Cell Aging in Relation to Stress Arousal and Cardiovascular Disease Risk Factors«, Psychoneuroendocrinology 31, no. 3 (April 2006): S. 277–287, doi:10.1016/j.psyneuen.2005.08.011.

evaluation situations are highly stressful. Here, too, there were differences: Some parents were able to deal with them better than others. What made the difference? What was the reason for this? The researchers concluded that there was one characteristic that led to carer parents doing better. Want to know what this trait was? Here we go: Challenge! [1] *People who see a stressful situation as a challenge, rather than a threat, cope better with stress.*

An amazing result! So, our mindset decides whether stress is going to undermine our body or not. In the following, I will introduce you to 3 different mindsets, all of which are very effective.

Growth mindset

"In every adversity lies a lesson and a blessing."
– Steve Harvey

This great Steve Harvey quote reflects this mindset. Anxiety and panic are opponents of life. Unfortunately, it doesn't help if we worry about our anxiety. It doesn't help if we are afraid of our panic. How about if we ask ourselves: What can I learn from this? And: Where is the blessing coming from my anxiety and panic? If we

---

[1] O'Donovan, A. J., et al., »Stress Appraisals and Cellular Aging: A Key Role for Anticipatory Threat in the Relationship Between Psychological Stress and Telomere Length«, Brain, Behavior, and Immunity 26, Nr. 4 (Mai 2012): S. 573–579, doi:10.1016/j.bbi.2012.01.007.

ask ourselves these questions, our condition will quickly improve. We don't focus on the problem but on the solution. We focus our attention on the positive and not on the negative. Now back to the question: What is positive about worries, fears and panic?

1 Worries, anxieties, and panic force us to develop further: If we are anxious, we have to develop wisdom and courage to overcome our anxieties. As we learned at the beginning of this book, Neo would never have grown to such greatness without his adversary Agent Smith. Anxieties make us courageous. They force us to gain wisdom.

2 Negative feelings are important for survival: Our brain is not interested in feeling good. No way! We are supposed to survive. Our brain is a survival expert. Our ancestors constantly had to fight off dangers like hunger, wild animals and accidents. Our ancestors could be attacked at any time by a tiger. Our brain had to be on guard: even the smallest sign was checked to see if it posed a threat. It was better to assess a harmless situation as dangerous than a dangerous circumstance as safe. So, our brain is virtually looking for dangers. In the past, it was essential for survival, today it is superfluous. Our world is quite safe. We are more likely to die of old age infirmity than from a tiger attack.

3. Signal for future threats: Another aspect is that emotions are signals. Fear tells us that there is the threat of something going wrong in the future. We may have to give a speech, but we are not yet ideally prepared. So, we should not just dismiss our negative feelings, but also look to see if there is something meaningful that they can tell us.

4. Signal for wrong thinking: Negative feelings are a signal that we believe untrue thoughts. This stems from cognitive behavioral therapy. Here's an example: Paula is afraid of flying: "The plane will definitely crash! I just saw on the news that a plane crashed." The thought that the plane would certainly crash is untrue. The probability of a plane crash is extremely low. This untrue thought frightens Paula. So, *angst* is a signal for an untrue thought. This is very interesting because it means that anxiety, worry, and panic are always based on untrue thoughts.

"Worries, anxiety and panic are always based on untrue thoughts."

How do we put a mindset like this into practice? The following exercise is a very effective way to integrate a mindset.

Power Person

Goal: Creation of a powerful condition, strengthening of the mindset

Technique

1. Stand up straight. Imagine in front of you a circle of flames. You can decide the color of the flames yourself. They are about 30 cm high. It is the circle of unlimited possibilities. Take a few deep breaths. Thank the circle and step inside.

2. Stand in the middle of the circle. Now imagine the Power Person. This is a person who is a role model for you. He stands in front of you.

Klaus suffered from panic. He had a panic attack about two to three times a week. He chose King Leonidas from the film 300 as his Power Person. For Klaus, King Leonidas embodied courage, strength, determination and clear thinking.

Say to the Power Person: "Give me your energy." Imagine how the energy flows from the Power Person to you. This energy fills your whole body. Feel how the qualities like courage and strength you receive from your Power Person grow within you.

Klaus imagined a thick beam of red light flowing to him from the middle of King Leonidas' chest. This red energy spread throughout his body. Klaus takes a powerful posture, clenches his fists and says loudly: "I am courageous, full of strength and determination! Klaus actually feels strong and courageous at this moment.

The goal is for you to actually feel the desired qualities, such as courage, strength, and determination. You have the energy! You can strengthen it by taking a correspondingly powerful posture.

4 Attract the Power Person to you, embrace them. Pull them closer and closer to you until they merge with your body. You have now taken over the qualities of your Power Person.

5. Breathe deeply a few times. Experience how you feel. Thank the circle and step out of it.

How often? How long? You can do this exercise any time when you need a boost of courage and strength. You can practice it in the morning to start the day because it puts you in a powerful state.

Tips & Tricks

- **Pick a Power Person** to help you defeat your fear. You can take a hero like Neo or Lara Croft. But you can also choose Buddha, the Dalai Lama or Jesus Christ. There are no limits. The main thing is that it feels good for you.
- **Following mindsets**: You can also use this exercise for the following mindsets.
- **Energy**: You can also imagine several energies. Klaus took a red energy beam. For example, you can imagine three energy rays, for each quality you want to take on: courage is red energy, joy is orange and clear thinking is blue. Again, visualize what feels good for you.
- **Several people**: You can also imagine several power people. Robert was afraid to speak to an audience. He imagined Anthony Robbins. In addition, he was shy, and it was difficult for him to get in touch with unknown people. That's why he imagined Barney Stinson from the series "How I met your Mother".
- **This ritual is extremely powerful** as visualizations,

38

affirmations and postures are used. The ritual is reinforced by actually stepping into the circle and embracing the Power Person.

The next mindset is also very supportive.

Mindset: The universe is friendly

"Reality is always much friendlier than any story we tell about it." – Byron Katie

This mindset is similar to the previous one. We can simply make the assumption that everything that happens to us has a friendly purpose. If we have fears, there is a positive intention behind them. The assumption we have about our world is important in terms of how we interpret our experience.

Max was a pessimist. For him, the world was a dangerous and unsafe place. He worked in the insurance industry. He didn't like his job at all: "I can't quit. That's far too insecure. What if I can't find a job? No, no, safety first." Max had developed many fears over time that limited him. He didn't fly: "The plane is bound to crash! Because he had the mindset that the world was dangerous, he lived full of fears and limitations. He focused his attention on them. He always had bad news: "Did you hear about the highway accident yesterday? 12 people died! In our first session, I introduced him to the mindset: "The universe is friendly". Max warded this off: "That is nonsense. Only yesterday there was a plane crash. Haven't you heard?" I replied: "Today the sun is shining. Spring is in the air and the sky is so beautifully blue. Have you noticed that? I philosophized further: "You can choose to focus your attention on the positive or the negative. Even with supposedly negative events, you can ask yourself, "What is positive about it?" We agreed that every night he would ask himself where exactly the universe had been friendly that day. His task was to find three examples. A week later, at our next session, Max was beaming, "I'm feeling better already. It is true, there is something positive about everything." In fact, Max was able to overcome his fears after some time.

The next mindset is not quite as obvious in its usefulness. For some people, it works great, for others, the first two mindsets are more suitable.

Mindset: Everything is ephemeral

I'd like to tell you a beautiful Sufi story first:

A king once questioned the wise men at his court and said to them, "I will have a beautiful ring made for me. I have the best diamonds you can get. I want to have a hidden message in the ring that can help me in times of total hopelessness. It must be very short so that it can be hidden under the diamond of the ring."

All the wise men, all the great scholars could have written long treatises about it. But to give him a message that contained only two or three words and would help him in times of great despair. They decided to consult their books, but they couldn't find anything. Now, the king had an old servant who was almost like a father to him. He had already been his father's servant. The king's mother had died early, and this servant had taken care of him. Therefore, he was not treated like a servant and the king had great respect for him.

The old man said: "I am not a wise man, I am not educated and not learned, but I know the message. There is only one message. These men cannot give it to you. Only a mystic, someone who has attained self-realization can give it to you.

During my long life in the palace, I have met all sorts of people, including a mystic. He was your father's guest, and I was assigned to him as a servant. When he left, he gave me this message as a gesture of gratitude for my services." And he wrote it on a small piece of paper, which he folded together, saying to the king, "Do not read it now. Keep it hidden in your ring and open it only when everything has failed when there is no other way out."

That time was about to come soon. The land had been invaded, and the king lost his kingdom. He had to flee on horseback to save his life and the enemy riders pursued him. He was alone; they were in the majority. He came to a place where he came to a standstill because the road had ended - he was standing on a cliff over a deep abyss. Falling down there would be the end of him. He could not go back because his enemies were there and he could already hear the hooves of their horses. He could not go forward and he had no way out.

Suddenly he remembered the ring. He opened it, took out the piece of paper, and on it was a short message of

41

very valuable meaning. It read: "This too shall pass." As he read the sentence, he became very still. "This too shall pass." And it did pass. Everything passes. Nothing is constant in this world. The enemies who had pursued him had probably lost their way in the forest, had probably taken the wrong path. After a while, he could no longer hear the sounds of their hooves.

The king felt enormous gratitude towards his servant and that unknown mystic. These words had worked like a miracle. He folded the piece of paper together again and put it back into the ring. He gathered his troops around him again and recaptured his empire. And the day he victoriously returned to his capital was celebrated throughout the city with music and dancing. He was very proud of himself.

The old man walked beside his carriage. He said: "Now it is the right moment again. Look at the message again." "What do you mean by that?" said the king. "Now I am victorious. The people are celebrating me. I'm not desperate. I'm not in a hopeless situation."

"Listen to me," said the old man. "This is what the saint told me then. This message is not only for times of despair, but it is also for times of joy. It is not only true for when you are the loser. It is also true when you are the victor. It is not only for when you are the last but also for when you are the first."

The king opened his ring and read the message: "This too shall pass. And suddenly he was overcome by the same peace, the same silence - in the midst of the crowd that was rejoicing, celebrating and dancing. His pride, his ego vanished. Everything passes away.

He asked his old servant to come into his carriage and sit next to him. He asked him: "Is there anything else? Everything passes... Your message has helped me tremendously." The old man said: "The third thing the wise man said to me back then was: Don't forget that everything passes. Only you remain. You remain forever as a witness."

A beautiful and touching story, isn't it? Everything is fleeting. Everything comes and goes. We are born, we live, we die. It is the same with our fears. They are fleeting. Even fear itself changes constantly. The next time you are afraid, try to feel it, feel how it changes. Everything changes, every second. Right now, at this moment, you are changing: Blood is being pumped through your veins, cells are dying, are being replaced by new cells, the air and water in your body are changing, your thoughts and feelings are changing, and so on. In the next second, you have already changed. Why is it important that we become aware of our transience?

- **Our lives are short.** Every minute, every second we are getting closer to our death. We don't know when we will die. Maybe it will be the day after tomorrow. When we realize how short our life is, that we can die at any time, we value our life more. Let us not waste our lives on anxiety. Let us grab the bull by the horns! Let us live - now!

  Imagine lying on your deathbed. You are going to die soon and you are looking back on your life. Has it been a good life? Were you brave and did you enjoy it? Or did you waste your life with worries and fears that didn't materialize anyway? What advice would your future self give you?

- **Feelings are also transient**: Especially people who suffer from panic attacks are often afraid that they will never stop. This is not true, of course. Panic is a survival program of the body to protect us from danger. When a tiger jumps out of the bushes, all the energies of the body are activated, enabling us to be able to run for our lives. Panic attacks last between 5 and 30 minutes. Panic is therefore of quite a short duration.

"When we are old and our days are counted - and that will happen any-way - only then will we realize that we never had anything to lose, be-cause we can choose the life we want to have." – Julia Engelmann

---

Which mindset do you like best? I suggest that you choose one first. Later, you can also use two or all three.

Three ways to integrate a mindset

These were three very effective mindsets. How can we put them into practice? There are three ways:

1. Power Person: This exercise is very empowering. It deepens the mindset and puts you in a powerful state.

44

You saw this technique above.

2. Three examples: In the evening, find three examples of your mindset. The more intensely and vividly you feel the situations, the better it is.

Alex has bushy, dark eyebrows and a deep, pleasant voice. He works as a real estate agent. He is successful in his job because he is very trustworthy and his voice is a great help. Although he can't actually complain, he has felt tired and listless for a few months now. He doesn't feel like going to work anymore. "My life is a treadmill - I do the same thing every day," he complains. We agree that he should use the mindset "The universe is friendly". His task was to write down some examples. That evening, Alex wrote: "Example 1: My lack of drive shows me that I should change something in my life. I should focus my attention more on the beautiful and the positive. Example 2: My work is not so bad at all! Today I have met such a nice couple. We got along well, told stories and laughed. I was able to sell them a nice, quite cheap apartment. I felt alive! Example 3: On the way home I noticed how beautiful the sunset was. Instead of just driving on, I stopped and looked at this beautiful scenery. It touched my heart." Alex's depressive mood disappeared after a short time.

3. Affirmations: You can create an affirmation for each mindset. For example, the growth mindset:

"I embrace challenges. I am persistent. I see effort as the way to mastery. I learn from criticism and failures."

For the second mindset, you can formulate the

following, for example:

"The universe is friendly. Everything that happens has a positive purpose. I see the good and the positive in everything."

On the third mindset, the following fits:

"Everything is transient. Negative things also pass. My life is short and I use and enjoy every minute and I don't waste time worrying and being afraid."

These are just examples. It is important that the affirmation feels good for you. You can recite the affirmations in the morning and evening. You can also use them on appropriate occasions. For example, if you are feeling discouraged or anxious.

Call to Action

Pick a method. You can stick with it or later if you have some experience with it, practice two or even all three methods at the same time. For example, in the morning you do the exercise "Power-Person", in the evening you do "Three Examples". In between, when you need some encouragement, you can practice affirmations.

Tip: There are great YouTube videos that are very motivating:
https://www.youtube.com/watch?v=wnHW6o8WMas,
https://www.youtube.com/watch?v=Q2FdfT3Qn_U or
http://bit.ly/1r0EUff. This is really powerful.

2.3 You must consider this forgotten factor if you want to get rid of your anxieties

"It is not death that a man should fear, but he should fear never beginning to live." – Marcus Aurelius

What you can look forward to in this chapter:

- Sport
- Meditation
- C.A.T.S.

Another important factor influencing anxiety is your general lifestyle.

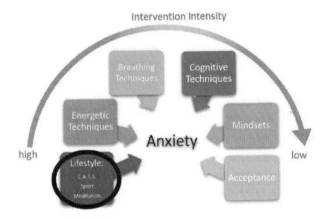

This factor is completely neglected in the vast majority of self-help books. People who suffer from anxiety often have an easily agitated nervous system. That is why we should make sure that we live a good life. What does that mean? Your general way of life can promote anxiety. If you have a lot of stress, sleep too little or party all the time, this can increase your susceptibility to anxiety. Stress, in particular favors fears. If you want to know how to reduce stress as easily as possible, I recommend my books: <u>Stress is a Decision</u> and <u>Stress is an Illusion</u>. Good, restful sleep is also important. Make sure you get between 7 and 8 hours of sleep.

In this section, I have chosen three particularly <u>important factors in our</u> lifestyle: Sport, meditation and C.A.T.S. Sport, and meditation have been proven to fight anxieties. They are also effective against stress and depression. C.A.T.S. is about other factors that promote anxiety. I have experienced some cases where fears simply disappeared by people taking care to avoid C.A.T.S.

Sport

There are thousands of studies that have proven the positive health effects of sport. The fact that sport also has positive effects on our satisfaction is not as well known. According to Hefferon, a professor of psychology at London University, sport has the following positive psychological effects:

- Anxiety, depression, and stress are reduced
- Overall performance increases, especially among children and older people
- Concentration and attention are improved
- The risk of dementia decreases
- Own body image improves

In addition, sport and exercise have innumerable positive effects on our body. For example, the risk of developing diseases such as cancer, diabetes or Alzheimer's is reduced. Fat is broken down, high blood pressure is lowered and bones are built up.

Amazing, isn't it? Now the question arises: How much exercise should I do to best ward off anxiety? To make it as easy as possible, I recommend taking at least 5,000 steps at least five times a week for three weeks. Exactly, taking a walk or walking is an excellent antidote for anxiety. The good thing is that just about anyone can walk.

For 5,000 steps, you need about 30 minutes, but you can spread it over the day. And yes, the way from the car to the supermarket also counts. Every path you take on foot counts. You can download an app on this.

There are a lot of free pedometers. You can also try several ones. It is important that the steps are counted quite accurately.

Call to Action

Start doing 5,000 steps first thing tomorrow. Best in the great outdoors. You'll see how good it does you. Rain or cold are no excuses - just make sure you are wearing the right clothing.

Body Scan: the optimal meditation for anxious people

Another method is meditation. It has an incredible number of positive effects. A lot of studies have been published, especially in recent times. If you want to know more about the advantages of meditation, have a look at this article: https://detlefbeeker.de/en/blog/really-need-meditate/ It has been scientifically proven that meditation is a wonderful remedy for anxiety.

There are many studies that prove that meditation is good for dealing with anxiety. But there was one study that I found particularly amazing. In the study, researchers found that meditation reduced the size of the amygdala. This is the fear and stress center of the brain. Isn't that amazing? Meditation visibly changes our brain! That means that we no longer react to situations so fearfully. Our thoughts are more positive (https://bit.ly/2eigk0h).

There are many different kinds of meditations. Breath meditations, formless meditations, analytical meditations, mantra meditations and many more. People who suffer from anxiety often have many thoughts. It is not easy for such people to be completely still and to tune in only to themselves because negative thoughts and feelings quickly emerge. This has to be considered when choosing meditation. Here, the Body Scan is optimal:

- The Body Scan keeps the mind very busy because we take our attention through the whole body. We start with the toes of the left foot, then the instep, the heel, and so on. In this way, we successively direct our attention to the whole body. Thus, we "scan" the whole physical body. In doing so, the thought-producing mind gets no opportunity to start coming up with any negative thoughts.
- If we are worriers and anxious people, we are

often tense. We pull up our shoulders and tense our muscles. With the Body Scan, we automatically relax when we focus our attention on a certain part of the body. Try it out right now: focus your attention on a part of your body that is currently tense. You will automatically relax these body parts. For these reasons, the Body Scan has a very calming and anxiety-relieving effect.

- From an energy perspective, there is another advantage: We stimulate our life force, or prana, and remove energy blocks. Why? Well, for example, when we focus our attention intensively on our left foot, we may notice a vibrating or tingling sensation. This is our life force. From many energy-based teachings, like yoga, we know the wisdom: *energy follows attention*. So, when we focus our attention on the life force during the Body Scan, the life force increases. From an energy or yogic point of view, this is a great advantage of Body Scanning.

"Energy follows attention."

What is the Body Scan?

The Body Scan is a great form of meditation. It has its origins in Buddhism and Hinduism.

The Body Scan is best known in connection with John Kabat-Zinn. He is an emeritus professor at the University of Massachusetts Medical School in Worcester.

He designed the famous MBSR (Mindfulness Based

Stress Reduction). This is an 8-week meditation program. The Body Scan is a central component. This program is tremendously effective with stress and anxiety and has featured in many studies.

There are different variants of the Body Scan: Yoga Nidra, an ancient yogic practice carried out long before the Body Scan was devised, is very well known. In yogic circles, Yoga Nidra is called yogic sleep. The Body Scan is based on Yoga Nidra but there are differences, e.g. at the beginning of Yoga Nidra, Sankalpa, a resolve, is made. This is a vision, a goal that the practitioner affirms inwardly several times. However, Yoga Nidra is an independent and comprehensive yogic system, while the Body Scan is merely a technique.

There are also distant Western relatives, such as autogenic training and progressive muscle relaxation. With autogenic training, the whole body is successively put into a state of relaxation with auto-suggestions and visualizations. In progressive muscle relaxation, for example, the practitioner successively first tenses the different parts of the body, for example, the right arm, then relaxes it. Then the left arm follows and so on with the rest of the parts of the body. So, the whole body is first tensed and then relaxed. This can actually achieve a deep state of relaxation in the physical body.

The Body Scan is especially suitable for beginners. Its effect is so relaxing because we focus our attention on different parts of the body. If our thoughts are reduced, tensions in the body are automatically released. As this form of meditation is done lying down, it is also very suitable for sleep disorders.

Compared to usual forms of meditation, which are carried out in a sitting position, the Body Scan has an advantage because a lot of people have problems sitting for a longer period of time, especially at the beginning. One part of the body may pinch and another may hurt. By contrast, the Body Scan takes no effort and also leads to deep relaxation.

Action Plan

Goal: Relaxation

Technique

Preparation:

- Lie down on your back. If you like, you can put a pillow under your head and also one under your knees. If you are in pain, you can also do the Body Scan lying on your side or sitting down. Close your eyes.
- Now take three deep breaths, breathing into your stomach.

Core Technique: During the Body Scan, your attention will move from one part of the body to another. You do two steps with each part of the body. Let's take the left big toe as an example:

1. Feel the life force in the left big toe. The life force expresses itself through fine vibrations and tingling. These are quite subtle. If you can't feel anything, don't worry.

Just take your attention inside the left big toe and become aware of any sensations inside the left big toe. The more you practice the Body Scan, the easier it will become for you to become aware of the life force in the different parts of the body as your attention moves from one part to another.

2 Breathe in and out in that part of your body, in this case, the left toe: Breathe in through your nose and imagine your breath flowing through your whole body, down to your left leg, then into your left foot and then into your left toe. Then, you breathe out from the left toe through your left leg, through your body and out of your nose.

Practice these two steps with each part of the body. You are moving your attention through the whole body and applying the two steps above. Start with the big left toe. Then continue with the remaining

four left toes

left foot

left lower leg

left knee

left thigh

right big toe

the remaining four right toes

right lower leg

right knee

54

right thigh

hip and pelvis

lower back

Abdomen and organs

upper back

thorax

left and right thumb and finger (simultaneously)

left and right hand

left and right forearm

left and right elbow

left and right upper arm

Shoulder and neck

face, head, and crown

How many times? How long? This meditation lasts about 30 minutes. You should do it at least three times a week. Daily is better.

Tips & Tricks

- **Download the Body Scan for free:** I learned the Body Scan myself with a spoken instruction. I found it very pleasant and relaxing. You can find spoken instruction here: https://detlefbeeker.de/body-scan/. I downloaded this audio onto my mobile phone. If I can't sleep, I'll listen to it and I'll travel to the land of dreams.

- **Falling asleep**: You can use the Body Scan is an excellent way of falling asleep. You have already practiced the Body Scan in the lying down position. I often inadvertently fall asleep while doing the Body Scan.

- **Beginning**: This meditation is especially suitable for the beginning because it is relaxing, but the mind is not left to its own devices. So, it's not so easy to start drifting into unfortunate stories.

- **Meditation has an incredible number of positive effects**. It is an all-rounder: you are calmer, stress is reduced, fears and also depression are reduced. On top of those blessings, your body can rejuvenate and your immune system is strengthened.

- **I often hear**: "Meditation is not for me. I'm too restless." Honestly? Everyone is initially restless in meditation. That's quite normal. And it is precisely *when* we find it difficult, that we should do the meditation. It's like our couch potato saying, "Jogging is not for me. It's way too exhausting." If it's too exhausting, our coach potato is out of shape and that is precisely *why* our coach potato *should* jog. The same thing applies to meditation. The more restless our "monkey mind" is, the more reason for us to meditate!

- **Thoughts**: If you digress, don't worry! It's completely normal. Although I have been meditating for many years, it still happens to me. Get back behind the steering wheel of the Body Scan and to being aware of the body.

- **There is no good or bad meditation**. We do not evaluate meditation. We already judge enough in everyday life. Meditation is an island of non-evaluation. If you follow the meditation instruction, then it automatically becomes a good meditation. Even if you're thinking a lot, no problem. That's what happens.
- **Important**: Stay with it. Don't break off the Body Scan in mid-stream. We are used to fleeing from our thoughts and negative feelings. We don't want to give them space. In meditation, we learn to face our thoughts and feelings. When fear appears, we still remain in meditation. The fear will then pass away again. So, we experience negative thoughts and feelings come and go.

Meditation is a protected space, so to speak. Fears can also arise in meditation. Since we are mindful in meditation, we can react differently from usual. We have our habitual reactions to fear. We usually let ourselves be drawn into our fear story.

"Yesterday, my boss looked at me in such a funny way. I haven't felt safe since the merger," Alfred complains. "Is he going to relocate me? Or is he thinking of firing me? I am already 51 years old, I will never find another job. I bet he's going to fire me. Oh my God! If he does, I will be on unemployment benefit and then I'll end up on the street! With these thoughts, it was understandable that he felt intense fear.

That's how it is when we get involved in the *angst* story.

In meditation, we deal with it differently: As soon as the first anxious thought comes up, we notice it because we are attentive. We simply return to the guidance and perception of our body. This nips anxiety in the bud. The crucial point is that we don't get drawn into the fear story. The more we train this in meditation, the easier it will be for us to do it in everyday life.

Call to Action

You're reading these lines right now. How about you meditate now? Don't lose time: Read the meditation instructions again, put down the book and meditate for five minutes. When you have done it, praise yourself for it. Pat yourself on the shoulder: "Well done!

"He who does not know anxiety is not courageous, he who knows anxiety is courageous and overcomes it."
– Khalil Gibran

If you bring sport and meditation into your life, it will have positive effects on many levels.

Download your free audio meditation

You will get an audio meditation from me as a gift. Under this link you can download it for free and without any obligation:

https://detlefbeeker.de/body-scan/

C.A.T.S

Believe it or not, food also causes anxiety and even panic. Some foods are known to promote anxiety and panic. Nevertheless, you should take a close look at when you experience anxiety and panic and whether it can be caused by food.

Roger had a sensitive stomach. For example, if he ate too much fat, it weighed heavily in his stomach. If he ate fat just before going to bed, he would have a panic attack at night. When he woke up, his heart was racing, and he got into a panic. Fortunately, he could easily prevent this panic by not eating anything greasy before going to bed.

Some foods promote our anxiety. It's a good idea to reduce their intake or to cut them out completely. They are called C.A.T.S. (Caffeine Alcohol Tobacco Sweetener):[1]

- **Caffeine**: If you suffer from anxiety, avoid caffeine. Even small doses can cause anxiety and even panic. Studies have shown that panic can be caused by caffeine. This depends on your genetic disposition. People who suffer from worries and anxieties are often physically tense, and this is ramped up by caffeine. Tension increases and so do worries and anxiety. Generally speaking,

---

[1] Wehrenberg (2008): *The 10 best-ever anxiety management techniques: understanding how your brain makes you anxious and what you can do to change it.*

caffeine can increase any form of anxiety. Even the smallest of doses can do this. Therefore, check your caffeine consumption! Coffee, energy drinks, tea, and chocolate? Yes, you are reading right. Even chocolate contains small amounts of caffeine.

- **Alcohol**: Many people use alcohol to relax. As a short-term effect, alcohol actually reduces anxiety and is relaxing. A few beers before going to bed can help you fall asleep. In phases of permanent stress, such as caring for a very sick person, people often permanently resort to alcohol. The only problem is that alcohol leaves the nervous system in an aroused state. So, if you drink alcohol before going to bed, you fall asleep faster. But you wake up after a few hours and can't fall asleep again. That's because of the alcohol. Because of its effect on the nervous system, alcohol is an anxiety stimulant. So, check out whether your alcohol consumption may be related to the fears you have. In general, it is a good idea to reduce your alcohol consumption.
- **Tobacco**: Smoking is known to have many health disadvantages. Nevertheless, smoking is perceived as relaxing: You take a little break when you smoke. This little ritual is relaxing. One withdraws from everyday stress and enjoys an attentive break. This is not due to smoking itself, but to the ritual attached to it. Nevertheless, tobacco consumption can cause anxiety. It may be that if you smoke only one cigarette, it is not a problem, but upwards of the third cigarette, it becomes

problematic. So, take a closer look at whether there might be a connection between fear and smoking in your life.

- **Sweeteners and sugar**: Sugar can also cause anxiety, as can artificial sweeteners. Not everyone is susceptible. Check this out for yourself. When you are anxious and did you priory consume sugar or a sweetener?

So, these were the usual suspects. Other foods can also cause anxiety and panic.

Call to Action

It's a good idea to keep a journal for a few days. Write down exactly when your fears occurred and what you ate or drank before. If you find a connection, so much the better! This is the easiest way to reduce fear and panic.

2.4 Warning: Your thoughts may be dangerous

"The only real enemies of human beings are their own negative thoughts." – Albert Einstein

What you can look forward to in this chapter:

- The Delete Button
- The Sedona Method
- The Work Plus

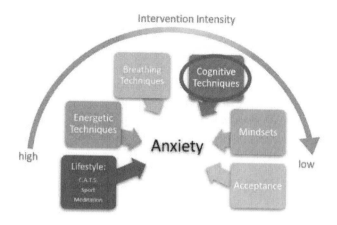

Anxious thoughts lead to anxiety. To find out if that is true, I have to backtrack a bit: Most people assume that events trigger our feelings. I didn't get the job and therefore I'm disappointed. My boss criticized me, so I am hurt and angry. My boyfriend/girlfriend cheated on me, so I am injured and angry. We can continue this list indefinitely. But is this really so? The clear answer is: No! It is the *thoughts* we have about a certain event that trigger our feelings.

The diagram shows this causal chain:

- First, we have the triggering situation. For example, our boss criticizes us.
- Now our thoughts and attitudes are added to this triggering situation. We think: "My boss is such an

ass! I've done everything well! Why does he criticize me? He doesn't like me! That is so unfair! I'll never get anywhere here." Such negative thoughts lead to negative feelings.

- The last step in the causal chain is emotion. We have negative thoughts and there is a feeling of anger or frustration.

Already 2000 years ago the former slave and great philosopher Epictetus realized:

"It is not the things themselves that upset us, but our beliefs about and our opinions of things." – Epictetus

Epictetus was born in 50 A.D. He was a slave in Rome. Life as a slave was very uncertain. He constantly lived in fear of being beaten or even killed. So, his master had his leg smashed. From that day on, Epictetus limped. To endure such a life was a challenge. Fortunately, when Epictetus was still a slave, he had access to Stoic teachings. Stoicism is a school of philosophy and is known for its adherents always staying calm. So, Epictetus realized that he could also be happy as a slave because not the events themselves made him suffer, but his attitudes and beliefs. Later, Epictetus was freed and founded his own school of philosophy. He is considered to be one of the greatest and most influential Stoics.

Is that good or bad? It's great! It means that you are independent of external events. If you lose your job, you can still be happy. If your partner breaks up with you,

you can still be in peace. All you have to do is change your beliefs and thoughts. This is much easier than changing the events. It is very difficult to get your partner to continue your relationship. Changing your beliefs is easy. This is the basis of cognitive behavioral therapy (CBT). It is a very effective form of therapy:

> *"Cognitive behavioral therapy is the most time- and cost effective psychotherapy for depression and anxiety."*
> *– Dr. Andrew Weil*

What has all this got to do with anxiety? Anxiety is triggered by fearful thoughts. That is why in this chapter I will introduce you to techniques that change your thoughts and reduce your anxiety.

If, for example, our partner leaves us, we think, "I will never find another partner again. I will be lonely and have no friends. At some point, I will die alone and the landlord will only find my corpse three weeks later". Anxieties arise from thoughts like these. That's what psychologists call catastrophizing. If we change our thoughts so that they are more rational, the fear will disappear.

Let me introduce you to three very effective ways of fighting anxiety. First, the Delete Button, a thought-stopping technique. It is simple and very effective. After that, you will get to know the Sedona method. It is impressively simple and has already helped hundreds of thousands of people. The next method is Work Plus. It examines whether your thoughts are really true. I have extended this method to include an effective element, especially for anxieties.

The Delete Button

Fears are caused by fearful thoughts. When we stop our thoughts, we also stop our fear. This is the idea of thought-stopping techniques. In the simplest version, we inwardly say to ourselves: "Stop! I'll present you with an improved version. Here, the thoughts are not only stopped but in addition, good feelings are generated. This is the premier class of thought-stopping techniques. The delete key has double the effect on fears compared to the classic thought-stopping technique.

Action Plan

Goal: Stop thinking and relax

Technique:

1. Imagine a button in the middle of your chest or in the palm of your hand that simply turns thinking off.

2 Successively inhale and exhale deeply three times into and out of your belly. Count the breaths and imagine a different color each time.

3. Now press the button and imagine your mind emptying itself completely. Make a movement with one hand as if you were actually pressing a button.

4. Focus your attention on the next two breaths and

gently bring your attention back to the present moment.

How often? How long? Do this exercise every time negative thoughts or feelings arise.

Tips & Tricks:

- **Persistence**: There is one catch: This exercise is not a quick fix. Your anxieties have been building up over many years, so they can't be eliminated in a few days. This means that you have to do the exercise consistently over and over again and over a longer period of time. This is the key to success. Practice the technique until the fears are gone or have clearly subsided so that you can accept them. This can take only one week, but if you are unlucky, it will take several weeks. Don't get discouraged - stay on the ball! You are bound to succeed!

- **Mindfulness**: In order to notice your negative thoughts and feelings staying attentive is a good idea. Keep on paying attention to yourself and your thoughts and feelings.

- **Baby Feelings:** Try to notice negative thoughts or feelings when they start to emerge. The smaller the thoughts and feelings are, the easier they are to fight.

- **Turbo Thought-Stopping:** Compared to the classic thought-stopping exercise, this improved version is much more effective. With the classic thought-stopping exercise, one simply thinks the word "stop". With the "Delete Button", we pay attention to our breath, imagine colors and visualize a Delete Button. In addition, we perform a small movement: We actually press the Delete Button. All this together makes up the enormous effect.

Joanna worries a lot. She is in her late 30s, tall with dark hair. Joanna works as a nurse in a local clinic. It's busy there at the moment It's winter. All the employees of the hospital are even more stressed than usual. "When will the holidays finally be over?", Joanna sighs: "I'm already sleeping badly because of all the stress." You're right," confirms her colleague, "I'm counting the seconds until the end of the day." The increased stress makes Joanna worry even more than usual. Her thoughts go round and round in circles: "I hope I won't lose my job! There are rumors that the hospital has no more money. Oh, I'm sleeping so badly, I'm bound to get depressed! In a coaching session, I introduced her to the Delete Button. "Try it out, you'll be surprised how well the technique works," I replied with conviction. "It can't hurt, I'll try the technique," Joanna said skeptically. No sooner said than done. She consistently applied the Delete Button to every negative thought or feeling she noticed. Of course, she also went through feelings. After a week, she felt much better. "I feel so much better", she beamed: "It's not only that I have fewer worries, but I am in a better mood than I was before. It almost seems like a mini-meditation to me".

Do you like the technique? The good thing is that it not

only stops your thoughts but also makes you feel better.

Call to Action

Apply the technique for the next hour to every negative thought and unpleasant feeling. When the hour is over, sum up. How do you feel? How often did you use the technique? Does the technique suit you?

Resources

The technique is described in the book "Mystic Cool" by Don Joseph Goewey. I really like the book because it contains a lot of great techniques.

The Sedona Method

This technique has already helped hundreds of thousands of people. We often hear that we should let go. But how exactly does that work? *How* do you let go? If it were that simple, we would have let go of all negativity long ago. This is where the Sedona method comes in. It was introduced by Hale Dwoskin in his bestselling book "The Sedona Method". He, in turn, adopted it from his teacher Lester Levenson. It's a technique that allows you to let go. The technique is simple and very effective. And it also works with our fears.

Action Plan

Goal: Relief from negative thoughts and anxieties

Technique

Focus on your issue and ask yourself these four questions:

1. Could I allow myself to welcome, allow, or be present with the feeling?

2. Could I let this feeling go?

3. Would I let go of this feeling?

4. When?

Repeat these four questions until you feel free of the feeling.

How long? How often? You can use this technique at any time when negative thoughts or feelings arise. So, it is an in-between technique. You can also use it preventatively in a quiet minute. After each round, tune in to yourself to see whether you have already let go of the feeling or of the thoughts. If not, keep on practicing the technique.

The changes may be subtle at first, but the more you repeat the questions, the more clearly you will feel how you are freeing yourself from the feeling.

Tips & Tricks:

- **From the heart**: Answer every question from your heart. Don't think too long. Surprisingly, your answer is not that important. Nothing that you do will be wrong.
- **Repeat**: Repeat the questions! You can repeat the questions until you have actually let go of the

feeling. Sometimes the four questions already work the first time. However, my experience is that I have to repeat the four questions several times and, depending on the intensity of the feeling, even more often. But that doesn't matter. I usually use the short form (see below).

- **There is no wrong answer**: You can freely answer the questions. I don't want to influence you, but I affirm the first question whereas I deny the second. I affirm the third again and the fourth...see below.

- **Out Loud or silently**: You can do this technique mentally or out loud. It works a bit better out loud.

- **Now**! The standard answer to question four "when?" is "now"! You can say "now" energetically or even really loudly. It should convince you.

- The technique even works without an answer: By the way, you don't *have to* answer the question. The questions look as if you do. But if you have time, then I recommend you to answer them.

- Short form: You can also do the whole technique in a short form. In that case, leave out the first question and ask yourself:

1. Could I let go of the feeling?
2. Would I?
3. When?

You don't always have enough time. If this is the

case, or if you are already very familiar with the process, you can do this short form. You only ask these 3 questions - it is not necessary to answer.

Everything O.K. so far? In the following, I will go deeper into the questions and how they work:

Explanations of the questions

Could I allow myself to welcome, allow, or be present with the feeling?

Acceptance is always a good idea. If we fight against fear or a feeling of worry, it becomes stronger. Accepting means that we give space to the feeling. This is not always easy, especially when the feeling is unpleasant. When I am afraid, I want the fear to go away. Inviting the fear doesn't look like a good idea. But resistance to feeling reinforces it. I like the image of the inner child: it is afraid. If we suppress the fear and want it to go away, the fear becomes stronger. Our inner child needs love. If we embrace it, it can let go of the fear. This immediately makes emotions softer and less intense.

Could I let go of this feeling?

Like with all questions, we should answer them from the heart. Just don't think too long. Letting go is not always so easy. Sometimes I can let go of an emotion easily, sometimes I can't. Everything is completely O.K. - any answer is O.K. Nevertheless, this question works. Our system is given the impulse to let go. That works very subtly.

Would I let go of this feeling?

Well, what can you answer? Of course, I want to let go of this feeling. This question reinforces the impulse given by the previous question.

When?

I answer this question every time with an energetic "now! This is the actual purpose of this question. We are brought back into the here and now.

The two ways to use the Sedona method

The Sedona method is flexible. We can use it either in an acute situation or preventively:

1. Letting go of current negative thoughts and feelings

Every time a worry/anxiety or negative thought appears, we can use the Sedona method. Suppose you are afraid of places and you approach one. You feel your anxiety appear. This is the perfect moment to use the Sedona method. Use the short form: "Could I let go of the fear? Would I? When? You can do this in thought.

You will see that your anxiety will quickly subside. Go a few rounds with the Sedona method until your anxiety has completely disappeared.

2. Preventively letting go of emotions

Paula is afraid of flying. She wants to fly to Dubai in two weeks. This is a six-hour flight. I advised Paula to use the Sedona method. She imagined the situation in detail, anxiety came up. Paula used the Sedona method. She needed several laps until the fear subsided. In the following couple of weeks, Paula practiced Sedona daily. As a result, her fear of flying had finally given way to a slight restlessness that Paula could tolerate well.

You can also use the Sedona method in written form. This means that you take a worry or fear and write down the beliefs and statements you have about it. Apply the Sedona method to each individual statement until you have let go of your worries or fears. You will be amazed at how well this method works.

If you want to work preventively, I recommend using the Sedona method in writing. In addition, you can use the method on other occasions. For example, when you drive to work: Meanwhile, you can simply use the four questions to work on your issues.

Carsten found the Sedona method practical. He had to drive a long way to get to work. He used the drive to work on his issues. He did this out loud: "Was I able to accept my anxiety about panic? Yes! Was I able to let it go? No! Would I? Yes! When? Now! He did the technique in a very committed way: He clenched his fists, talked loudly and firmly. He repeated the questions many times until he felt an improvement. For stubborn topics, such as his fear of panic, he had to do more laps than for easier ones. "The technique works great," he told me, "but sometimes, especially on difficult topics, I have to start all over again the next day. Yesterday, I worked the whole way back on my "fear of panic" issue. I felt that the fear was diminishing. That felt great. Today the fear was stronger again and I had to practice Sedona many times." "Was the fear as strong as yesterday when you started," I asked. "No, it was weaker, but still stronger compared to the intensity when I stopped yesterday," Carsten replied. "That's not bad at all and does happen, especially with persistent topics. They like to come back. Here, the motto is: "Pass through". It gets better each time, and soon the fear is completely gone." In fact, Carsten was able to free himself from his fear of panic.

The Sedona method usually works very quickly, but it takes a little longer for particularly persistent topics. The method is not a quick fix, but it is very powerful and can free you from your anxieties.

Call to Action

The Sedona method has a huge advantage: you can use it at any time. Use the Sedona method for one week at idle times. You stand in a queue and have nothing to do? Practice Sedona! Do you drive a car? Practice Sedona. Are you going for a walk? An excellent opportunity to practice Sedona. Make a list of the topics you would like to work on. Carry it with you so that you always have a theme. You can work on any topic: your fear of panic, your worries about your job, your anger towards your partner, your desire for sweets, etc.

Resources

The Sedona method is explained very well in the basic work "The Sedona Method: How to free yourself from emotional baggage and realize your wishes in 5 easy steps" by Hale Dwoskin. Do you like watching videos? The following is a link to a YouTube video: https://www.youtube.com/watch?v=w2sZpCWeHtU.

The Work Plus

The Work was developed by Byron Katie. She suffered from such severe anxiety and depression, that she could hardly leave her bed. She reported that she experienced enlightenment that completely freed her from her fear and depression. She developed The Work in order to teach her fellow human beings how to achieve inner peace.

This method is incredibly effective. After using it the first time, you will notice a difference.

I have added an element to this method which makes it easier to deal with anxieties.

Action Plan

Goal: Dissolving negative thoughts and anxieties

Technique

Step 1: The first step is to find out what your beliefs and negative thoughts about the situation are.

Worries and fears relate to the future. We are afraid that something will go wrong in the future. When fears and panic arise, the following beliefs often come into play:

- **Probability overestimation**: the occurrence of negative events is completely overestimated. Paula is afraid of flying. The probability of her plane crashing is extremely low. Paula, however, assumes a much higher probability. This is what causes her fear of flying.

  Fred is afraid of losing his job. He lost his two previous jobs and has developed this fear. In fact, there was no danger. I advised him to work on his fears with The Work. His belief was: "I'm going to lose my job. That's terrible." On The Work's first question, Fred could see that he couldn't know whether he was going to lose his job. That helped him, but not completely. I advised him to assess the likelihood that he was going to be dismissed.

He was asked to fill out the following brief form[1]:

What is the negative event that I predict will happen?			"*I'm gonna lose my job*"						
In reality, how likely is it that this negative event will occur?									
1	2	~~3~~	4	5	6	7	8	9	10
Absolutely unlikely		highly unlikely		approx. 50% probability of occurrence		very likely		almost certain	

Fred crossed Box "3". It is important that we fill out this form in writing and not just in our heads. Fred was able to concretely see that this probability was very low. That gave him a lot of relief.

If you have a fear, then this little form can be very helpful. It is important that you actually do it in writing. That always has a stronger effect than if you only clarify it in your head.

- **Catastrophization**: In our fantasy world, we imagine the future much worse than it will actually be. Kevin was afraid of loss. He imagined that if his girlfriend Lisa left him, he would never find another girlfriend and die lonely, abandoned and sad.

People who suffer from panic often have the catastrophic idea that their panic will never stop. Of course, this is not the case. Panic passes. On

---

[1] I took this form from the book, Cognitive Behavioural Therapy Workbook for Dummies

average, panic lasts no longer than 20 minutes.

- **Unpleasant vs. awful**: our assessment of the situation is important. It influences how we experience this situation and what feelings occur. People who suffer from anxiety tend to quickly perceive situations as awful.

Stefan suffered from fears. Physically speaking, they were especially noticeable in the solar plexus. We talked about his unpleasant mindset. "How about you classify your fear as unpleasant," I challenged him. He replied: "What? You don't even know what it's like. I feel terrible, an unpleasant feeling develops especially in the pit of my stomach." "It is terrible to get cancer, to be tortured. Is it really that bad to have an unpleasant feeling in your stomach pit? Is it really that important? Decide to say your angst is unpleasant." Stefan became thoughtful: "Yes, you're right, I'll try." In the next week, his suffering had already diminished considerably. "My anxiety is just unpleasant! I am so happy," he announced.

In truth, most things are just unpleasant. Angst is unpleasant, but not really awful. Even panic is unpleasant, but is it really terrible? Losing a leg in a car accident is awful. Panic lasts only a few minutes. It is a sensation. Is it really awful? If we train ourselves to simply regard events as unpleasant, we can be more relaxed with them.

A friend of mine is an expert in martial arts. He

teaches self-defense courses. He used to work in the army and has lived in the most extreme conditions. He has jumped parachutes, done survival training and used to be a combat diver. In addition, he is trained in many fighting techniques and has boxed full contact. So, he is a tough guy. I always experience him as being calm. He says, "I've experienced so many really life-threatening situations that everyday things like being late or even losing my job don't upset me at all. I know it doesn't matter." Isn't he right?

These were a few suggestions that will help you to find your beliefs or thoughts. The rule of thumb is: "The more intense the anxiety, the hotter the thoughts". So, if your *angst* is intense, your thoughts will also be intense.

Carl was afraid of losing his job. He was very concerned about that. He thought: "My boss is going to fire me! They'll kick me out. I won't find another job at my age. I'll lose my apartment and end up on the streets." In fact, Carl was not facing any real threat. He overestimated the likelihood that this negative event would happen. Then he catastrophized. Why shouldn't he find a new job? Fearing that he would end up on the streets is also catastrophizing

Step 2 - Detective: We are now going to play detective and we want to find out if our questions are really true. Often, we automatically assume that our thoughts are true. This causes a lot of suffering. Therefore, it is important to have the following attitude:

"Every thought is an assertion."

This attitude takes the power out of the thought. It is now our job to prove whether the thought is true or false.

We ask four questions on each of these statements and reverse them. At first glance, this sounds like a lot of work. But it is not. Often it is sufficient to work on two or three statements intensively. The rest is self-evident.

Let's take Carl's statement: *"My boss is going to fire me!"* The first question we ask ourselves is this:

1. Is that true? We go inside ourselves and respond from the heart. I.e. we do not give a quick mind answer, but instead, we work on this question.

Carl replied: "Of course this is true! Every answer is correct. This is not about censoring or finding the right answer.

2. Can you really know one hundred percent that it's true? You're right, it's the same question again. That's because we tend to answer the first question too quickly.

The second question made Carl think more. He said: "Well, actually I can't really know. My company is doing well, nobody has been fired for a long time. As well as that, I'm doing a good job, so there's no reason for me to get fired."

As an alternative question, you can also ask: **Where is the proof?**

It's interesting to analyze the **worst-case scenario:**

Would it really be so bad if Carl became unemployed, couldn't find a job and lost his apartment? That would be the worst case. Carl wouldn't end up on the streets because he has friends. He would stay with friends for a short time and look for a new apartment. Of course, all this is not pleasant. Being unemployed is not pleasant. You have to be very careful with your money. But that does not automatically mean that you are unhappy. There are a lot of people who have little money but are satisfied. There are also people who are very rich and dissatisfied.

If we face the worst-case scenario and realize that it's not so bad, that can give us a lot of inner peace.

The first two questions are about softening our negative thoughts. Negative thoughts do not necessarily cause negative feelings. It is only when we believe negative thoughts that they gain strength and then negative feelings arise. If I think I will die of cancer but don't believe it, the thought has no meaning. By asking: "Is that thought really true?" we are expressing our doubts about the truth of the thought. Maybe this thought is not true at all. If we don't believe the negative thought, it won't do us any harm. Between you and me: Most negative thoughts are not true. If you do The Work more frequently, you will most likely also come to this conclusion.

"If we don't believe negative thoughts, they don't do us any harm."

---

3. How do I react to this thought? What do we feel and how do we act when we think this thought?

Regarding our example: "How does Carl react to the thought that he will lose his job? This means feelings and actions. Carl feels afraid. He is restless inside and feels stressed in his job.

4 What would I be without this thought? I'm a big fan of the Harry Potter movies. Do you know the scene where Dumbledore pulls a thought out of his head with his magic wand? It's exactly the same here: Imagine you couldn't think that thought. How would that be?

Carl answers: "I would be much more relaxed in my job. I would just do my job. I would also be less restless and anxious overall, and could enjoy my life more".

The fourth question leads straight to the realization that it is not the actual events that lead us, but our thoughts. This is a wonderful realization.

"It's not what happens that makes us feel bad, it's our beliefs and thoughts about what happens."

The turnaround

With the first two questions, we can see that our negative thoughts are not true. Questions three and four lead us to the realization that it is not the situation that makes us feel bad, but it is our negative thoughts that make us feel bad. The turnaround goes one step further: our negative thoughts are reversed here. We

82

realize that the opposite of our negative thoughts is true. Let's look at Carl's example. There are several ways of doing the turnaround:

1. Is the opposite truer?

The opposite is truer: "My boss is not going to fire me!" Is that true? Yes! It is much more likely that Carl will keep his job. There is no reason for him to be fired.

2. Put yourself into the picture:

Instead of saying "my boss is going to fire me, the reversal is "I am firing myself!" When doing the turnaround, always ask yourself if it's truer than the original statement. In a figurative sense, Carl is firing himself. Why? Because in his mind he has fired himself thousands of times. In this respect, this turnaround is also true. Allow the particular reversal to affect you and then decide whether it fits.

3. Insert my thinking:

Here, the turnaround is: "My thinking fires me!" In this case, it is similar to the previous reversal. Is this reversal truer than the original statement? Yes! Carl has often fired himself in his mind. So, this turnaround is truer than the original thought.

4. Reversal:

Probably not. The turnaround is: "Carl is firing his boss!" Is that truer than the original statement? This reversal is more difficult. It doesn't fit.

You don't always have to make all four reversals. It is enough if we find one that seems truer to us than the original statement. The turnaround should touch us and make it clear how one-sidedly we have judged the situation. It should create an "ah-ha" experience for us.

Step 3 - Affirmations: This is the "plus" of The Work Plus. This step was developed by me especially for working with fears. For anxiety and panic, it's good to have fast-acting means, like affirmations. The Work is an excellent accompaniment to affirmations, because we can find out exactly what the counter-thoughts are that bring us relaxation by intensively dealing with our thoughts.

In this step, we find affirmation. Affirmations are sentences that calm you down or give you strength. You can apply them to all possible levels and areas of life. They give your mind a positive direction. Instead of negative self-talk, you now have positive self-talk that builds you up and strengthens you. If, for example, you are afraid of flying, you can affirm: "When I fly, I am safe and secure".

When you set up your affirmations, you should consider the following points:

1. Affirmations should be formulated in the present tense form, for example: "I am calm and relaxed".

2. Affirmations should be positive. So, don't: "I'm not afraid". It is better to say: "I am safe and completely relaxed".

3. Affirmations should reflect the facts. Affirmations carry a danger of reinforcing the negative.

Joe was heavily overweight. He considered the

affirmation: "I am thin". That just wasn't true and Joe knew that of course. Every time he practiced this affirmation, it reminded him that he was overweight. This affirmation had an unfavorable effect.

Therefore, it is important that an affirmation is factual. So, if we are afraid that panic won't go away, we can realistically affirm: " Anxiety comes and goes". This is a helpful and believable affirmation.

Carl, for example, could affirm: "I will keep my job. I do a good job and there's no reason for me to lose it. I'm also protected from dismissal."

The purpose of these affirmations is to counteract negative thoughts. If we have time, we can do the complete The Work, if we have less time, let's just say the affirmation. This calms us down and our fears are reduced. You can also use the affirmations preventively. For example, you can recite your affirmations in the morning.

Affirmations can consist of only one sentence or a small text. The main thing is that they work.

How many times? How long? Work with the affirmations for about three weeks. Then see if and how they are working. If necessary, you can change and adapt the affirmations.

Tips & Tricks:

- **Booster #1**: You can boost the effectiveness of the affirmations by writing them down. Every morning, grab a pen and paper and write down your affirmation. This is more powerful than just thinking or reciting your affirmation.

- **Booster #2**: Another way to boost your affirmations is to stand in front of a mirror. Look into your eyes and say the affirmation. The best time to do this is in the morning.
- **Booster #3**: You can increase the effectiveness of the affirmations by reciting them as passionately as possible. You can clench your fists and take a strong posture.
- **You can create affirmations yourself.** But you can also search the Internet for them and get inspired. You can find a good list under the following link: https://www.developgoodhabits.com/positive-affirmations/
- **Affirmations for anxiety**: Here, the affirmations are meant to be used for anxieties. This will calm you down quickly.
- **You can change and customize the affirmation at any time**. Feel inside yourself if the affirmation is right for you in this particular situation. An affirmation may sound beautiful, but it is important that it fits with you.

How often? How long? I recommend that you make a "The-Work"-Bootcamp. This means that you apply The Work daily in writing, preferably in the evening. Do that for three weeks. I.e. you sit down in the evening and take one or more situations that gave you negative feelings. You investigate them with The Work. Important: You should do this in writing. This takes about 15 minutes. You do these sessions daily for three weeks. This will re-program yourself. You will learn to see and evaluate situations differently. You will experience more and more inner peace. The good thing is that you only need to do this boot camp once in your life.

Then apply The Work whenever negative feelings occur. If you are already very confident, you can do it in your head rather than in writing. But that should be more of an exception. Otherwise, you should use The Work one to three times a week in writing.

Tips & Tricks

- **Written**: The Work is really a great method. It leads to inner peace. You should use it regularly and this is important: It must be done in written form!
- **Answer questions freshly**: The questions should not be answered mechanically. I know from my own experience: If you have more experience with The Work, you tend to answer the questions quickly because you already know the answers. I usually know that negative thought is not true. And I know that the negative thought leads me to negative feelings. Nevertheless, we should always answer the questions freshly, as if it were the first time.
- **Who is in control here**? Ask this question as the fifth question! It is very effective. It does not belong to the original The Work, but it is a useful addition. The following example describes how you deal with this question.
- **Three examples in the turnaround**: In the turnaround, you can also find three examples that support each turnaround. This increases the

effect.

One turnaround was: "My boss won't fire me". He can now find three reasons or examples of this. One reason would be: "I'm doing a good job." Second reason: "The company is doing well, there's no reason to fire me." Third reason: "I'm protected against dismissal."

Let's look at another example.

The negative thought is, "I'll die of my panic."

1. Is it true? And where is the proof? Many people suffer from panic. No one has ever died of it. That is also not the sense of panic: Panic is supposed to protect us in dangerous situations. I.e., if a tiger jumps from the grass and threatens our life, we should have enough energy to flee from it. That is panic. It is a survival program. So, exactly the opposite of pathological panic. Therefore, we conclude: "It is not true."

2. Is it really true? No! If we came to this conclusion already in the first question, we don't need to answer the second one again.

4. How do I react to this thought? We develop anxiety about panic. That makes things even worse. We are restless and anxious.

5. Who would I be without this thought? I would simply be in the here and now. I would not be afraid of panic. I would live in the moment. All in all, I would be more relaxed.

The turnaround:

Here the turnaround fits best: "I won't die." Because this is truer than the original statement. Panic is a survival and not a dying program.

Affirmations: "Panic is a survival program of the body. I have not died of my panic yet and no one has died yet. Panic only lasts a few minutes and nothing really happens. It's not worth being afraid of it."

I hope that the example has made you more familiar with the method. This method is really worth using.

Call to Action

Take any worry or fear and find out what the underlying beliefs are. You should start with a feeling that has only a slight intensity, otherwise, it can be too upsetting. Apply The Work to these beliefs. Then make an affirmation.

Resources

Want to know more? The following books and hints are real gems:

- The "bible" of this method is by its founder: *Byron Katie: Love What Is*. It is a great book with many examples.
- There are lots of videos worth seeing on YouTube. I highly recommend videos by Byron Katie. Just type her name in the search box on YouTube and you'll get lots of great videos.
- Ellis (2006): *How you stubbornly refuse to be*

unhappy. This book is by Dr. Albert Ellis. He is one of the founders of cognitive behavioral therapy. This book will change your life. It's not The Work, but it explains a very similar concept, the ABCD model.

That's it on cognitive techniques. Did you like them? They really are very effective and they constitute an important part of this book.

2.5 Three effective anti-anxiety switches

"The quality of breathing determines the quality of life."
– Paracelsus

What you can look forward to in this chapter:

- 4-7-8 breathing has been shown to be stronger than anxiety-dissipating drugs.
- BELL uses deep breath, smiles and conscious body relaxation
- Anti-panic breathing is the bazooka among breathing techniques.

Breathing techniques work quickly with all kinds of fears. That's why I called them anti-anxiety switches. When we are afraid, when we worry or panic, we hold our breath or breathe shallowly and fast. If we breathe deeply and slowly, it sends signals to our brain telling it that there is no danger. Fear is automatically relieved. We should use this mechanism. In this book, I present three breathing techniques:

- **4-7-8 Breathing**: This was developed by Dr.

Andrew Weil. It is very calming and has become very well-known. It has been proven to be more effective against anxiety and panic than medication.

- **Anti-Panic Breathing**: This is based on 4-7-8 breathing, but contains some more powerful elements. It was specially developed to combat panic. It is extremely powerful. However, it requires training because it is not so simple.
- **BELL** is another powerful breathing technique. Anxiety often makes us tense. It's important to cultivate relaxation. This automatically reduces anxiety. BELL is very easy to use and works fast.

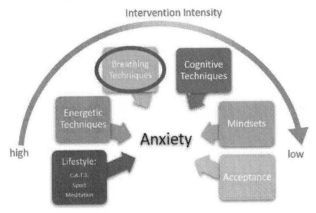

4-7-8 breathing: sleeping in 60 seconds

"The strongest and most effective anti-anxiety treatment I know is the 4-7-8 breathing technique. I have seen it work on the most extreme forms of panic disorder when the strongest medications have failed."

91

This breathing technique was propagated by Dr. Andrew Weil. It is a great remedy for anxiety and stress. Performed daily, this breathing has other positive effects, such as a significant reduction of blood pressure or lowering of the average heart rate. This breathing technique is so effective that it even works better than medication when it comes to combatting fears and panic attacks. This breathing technique is famous for its effectiveness in combating sleep problems. According to Dr. Weil, it takes only 60 seconds to fall asleep if we use this technique. I have tried it myself and this is true. It is a simple and very effective, relaxation breathing technique. It has other advantages besides relaxation:

"The benefits are gradual and cumulative, which ultimately leads to better health for the entire nervous system. It is also a specific treatment for hypertension, cold hands, irritable bowel syndrome, arrhythmia, anxiety and panic disorders, and a variety of other common conditions. Above all, it is the most effective and time-efficient relaxation method I have found." – Dr. Weil

---

Action plan

Goal: Relaxation, anxiety reduction

Technique:

Preparation:

- Touch your palate with the tip of your tongue, just behind the upper incisors. Keep your tongue in this position throughout breathing. This will prevent your mouth from drying out.
- Breathe out completely through your mouth and sharpened lips, with a whooshing sound, as if you wanted to blow out birthday candles.

The actual technique:

1. Close your mouth and inhale silently through your nose, counting to four.

2. Hold your breath, counting to seven.

3. Exhale through your mouth as if you were blowing out birthday candles, counting to eight.

Repeat Steps 1 to 3 for a total of four breaths.

How often? How long? At least twice a day. In addition, every time negative thoughts or feelings arise. For the first four weeks, don't take more than four breaths each time. After that, you are welcome to do more.

Tips & Tricks:

- **Morning and evening**: You can use the breathing at any time. Dr. Weil himself recommends using it in the morning after waking up and in the evening before going to bed.
- **Sleep in one minute**: Breathing is known to let you fall asleep in one minute. So, if you have sleep problems, this technique is the best help.
- **Keep the ratio**: The total number of seconds it takes to breathe is less important than maintaining the ratio. A person who cannot hold their breath long enough can try a shorter pattern instead, such as

  breathe in through the nose for a count of 2 seconds, hold the breath for a count of 3.5 seconds, exhale through the mouth for a count of 4 seconds

  As long as you maintain the right ratio, everything will be perfect and 4-7-8 breathing will take full effect.
- According to some proponents of 4-7-8 breathing, the longer and more often the technique is used, the more effective it becomes.
- In rare cases, in the beginning, you may feel dizzy. It is therefore advisable to try this technique while sitting or lying down in order to avoid dizziness and falls.

Patrick was stressed. The main cause was his work. His

department was understaffed, so Patrick often had to work overtime. Projects were particularly tugging at his nerves and often had to be completed in far too short a time. He already had the first symptoms of stress: sleep problems, nervousness, and occasional anxiety. He used 4-7-8 breathing every morning and evening. "I just don't have time to meditate," he said, explaining his decision. He also used the breathing technique when he noticed that it was all too much for him and he was getting nervous. Already after a few days, he noticed an improvement.

Call to Action

Practice this breathing technique for one week every morning after getting up and every evening before falling asleep. Then take some time to see if anything has changed. Have you calmed down?

Resources

Dr. Weil explains the breathing technique in a video under the following link: https://www.youtube.com/watch?v=gz4G31LGyog. You can find the technique in Andrew Weil's book: "Spontaneous Happiness".

Anti-Panic Breathing (APB): the secret weapon against panic

The next technique I would like to introduce you to is a very powerful and effective breathing technique that you can use especially for panic. Of course, you can also use it for milder anxieties. APB is also excellent for building up energy. So, if you're tired and need a little energy boost, APB is a good choice. The breathing technique is a combination of three very effective techniques:

The first is **4-7-8 breathing**, which in itself is excellent for fear and panic. This is combined with another technique that works on an energetic level: **Kundalini Yoga**. The third building block is from Energy Psychology. You will learn more about this in the next chapter. There, I will also introduce you to a particularly effective method: Eutaptics. APB is demanding. But with some practice, you will master it easily. That means, if you suffer from panic attacks, you should practice this breathing only in quiet moments.

Action plan

Goal: reduction of panic, relaxation, energy boost

Technique

APB is very powerful against panic but is not an easy technique. That's why I have divided it into several steps.

Step 1: 4-7-8 Breathing

In this first step, you practice the 4-7-8 breathing. By itself, it is very effective in combatting fears and panic. There are scientific studies showing that 4-7-8 breathing is more effective against anxiety and panic than medication. You have already learned this breathing above, but we will repeat it briefly:

- Close your mouth and inhale silently through your nose, for the count of four. Place the tip of your tongue on your palate behind your incisors.
- Hold your breath for the count of seven.
- Breathe out through your mouth as if you were blowing out birthday candles, for the count of eight.
- Repeat this cycle four times.

That's it. In the next step, we add another element.

Step 2: 4-7-8 + Kundalini

In this step, an element from kundalini yoga, namely the anus, is added. This element creates energy that goes up the spine.

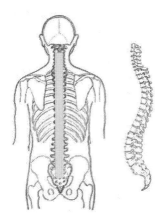

Energy techniques work very well against panic. During a panic attack, it is not always possible to perform subtle techniques, but the anus can be tightened even during a panic attack.

- Close your mouth and inhale silently through your nose, for the count of four.
- Hold your breath and count to seven. **Contract your anus firmly**. Make sure your spine is straight.
- Breathe out through your mouth as if you were blowing out birthday candles, for the count of eight. **Relax the tension in your anus.**
- Repeat this cycle for a total of four breaths.

Step 3: 4-7-8 + Kundalini + EFT

Now, we add one more element from energy psychology, the EFT (Emotional Freedom Technique). This method works with acupuncture points to control mental ailments such as anxiety or depression using energy techniques. We use two emergency points to help in extreme emotional situations: The hand edge point and the clavicle point. You tap these in addition to the techniques already practiced.

- Close your mouth and inhale silently through your nose on the count of four. **Tap on the outer edge of the hand**. Tap firmly on the edge of your hand with four fingers (see picture):

- Hold your breath, for the counting of seven. Contract your anus firmly. **Tap the outer edge of your hand**.
- Breathe out through your mouth as if you were blowing out birthday candles, counting to eight. Let go of the tension in your anus. **Tap on the outer edge of your hand**.
- Repeat this cycle for a total of four breaths. In the 2nd cycle, you then tap the **clavicle point(s)**. You can tap only one or both points.

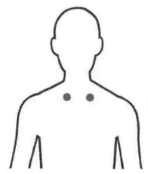

clavicle points
(The point is located in the hollow under the clavicle, where it merges into the sternum.)

- In the 3rd cycle, again tap the hand outer edge point and in the 4th cycle, again tap the clavicle point.

That was APB. APB consists of all three steps simultaneously. This technique is incredibly powerful. At first, it seems complicated, but once you've practiced it a few times, it won't be a problem anymore.

How often? How long? Every time a panic attack arises. You do each cycle four times. The panic attack is normally significantly alleviated, or even completely disappears. If not, just keep practicing APB until the panic attack is over.

Tips & Tricks:

- **This breathing technique is incredibly powerful against panic attacks**. The 4-7-8 breathing, in itself, is very good and effective against anxiety and panic. This breathing technique here is the suped-up version, the anti-panic turbo version, so to speak.

- **In addition to the 4-7-8 breathing, there are several elements**: 1. You contract your anus while holding your breath. This is a technique from kundalini yoga. This is also an energizing element. 2. The emergency points from EFT are also used.
- **Learn in Steps**: If you practice this breathing technique, begin to contract your anus while holding the breath, and do so vigorously. If you have internalized this, then add tapping. It all may sound complicated, but it's not. After a few times, you'll get the hang of it. And then you will have a technique that will help you during the panic attack.
- **Baby Feelings**: Try to get the panic under control as you climb up. As a baby feeling, it's easier to control it. When you then do the breathing, everything is quickly released.
- **Tip**: Many people who are affected by panic attacks are afraid that the panic attack will not stop. That's not true, of course. Panic is an extreme alarm condition of the body. It can't be sustained for long. That's why you don't have to worry. The panic attack definitely will pass. And it will also pass without any techniques at all.

Fred had a panic disorder. In a coaching session, I had shown him the anti-panic breathing. "You have to practice it because when you are in the middle of a panic attack, it's very hard to do anything at all. In other words, you must get the technique right and be able to do it in your sleep," I warned. "All right, I will," Fred replied. He had one or two panic attacks a week. Two days after the session, he had the next one. It overcame him immediately after getting up. Fred inhaled for four seconds and tapped the first emergency point (hand edge point). He held his breath for seven seconds, contracting his sphincter muscle. Then he breathed out for eight seconds through his mouth, as if he wanted to blow out birthday candles. He couldn't remember the second emergency point in the hectic of the action, so he only tapped the edge of his hand. "I can't remember exactly, but I think I breathed six rounds of APB. Then the panic eased. I was so relieved," he confessed to me in the next session, "for the first time I felt that I had my panic under control. "You did a great job. It doesn't matter that you left out the clavicle point - it worked anyway. Still: Train your breathing a bit more so that you can do it in your sleep because panic is an extreme situation," I explained. With the help of anti-panic breathing, Fred was able to almost eliminate his panic within a few weeks.

You can fight your panic very effectively with the help of APB. This is important: Stay tuned! It's worth it!

Call to Action

Decide to practice the technique for a week. If a panic attack occurs, it is important that you can do the exercise in your sleep.

Monday: Do the 4-7-8 breathing 10 times a day.

Tuesday and Wednesday: Practice 10 x 4-7-8 breathing and contract your anus while holding your breath.

Thursday and Friday: Now add the tapping of the

meridian points. And practice breathing 10 times.

Saturday and Sunday: On these days, practice the full breathing 10 times. You will see how well you feel after APB.

You will get to know BELL, below. It is always applicable and only takes a few seconds.

BELL

BELL is also a breathing technique. They all work great against fears. Why? Because we breathe faster when we are experiencing fear. When we start the antidote program - slow and deep breathing - it sends a signal to our brain that there is no danger. Our system can calm down. BELL adds further elements so that it is even more effective against anxiety. The technique has a re-laxing effect and creates a good mood. So, you can use it not only against fears but at any time if you need some relaxation or want to get into a good mood. This mindfulness technique involves smiling and a brief re-lease of all tension. Therefore, it is very relaxing within a short space of time.

"BELL" means bell. This means the dharma bell. In Buddhist monasteries, a bell is rung at irregular intervals. At the sound of the bell, all monks pause and become attentive. The bell is a reminder.

Action Plan

Goal: Quick relaxation, works against negative feelings, mindfulness

Technique

BELL is an acronym. Each letter of the word represents one step in the technique.

B = Breathing: Breathe deeply into the abdomen through the nose so that it bulges outwards. This sends a signal to the brain that there is no danger. Because in the case of anxiety and stress, we breathe flatly and quickly into the chest. That is why deep abdominal breathing is a great antidote to anxiety and stress.

E = rElax your body: When you exhale, drop your shoulders and briefly relax all your muscles. At first, it is enough to just drop your shoulders. This is because often our tension is in our shoulders and neck. The goal, after some practice, should be to scan your entire body briefly and relax all your muscles at once. With a little practice, this can be done very quickly. We tense up when we are afraid and stressed. Conscious relaxation works wonderfully against fears and stress.

L = Laugh: Laugh out as loud, or smile as broadly, as possible. Show your teeth! You don't have to feel like smiling. Smiling always has a relaxing effect, whether you are faking it or not.

L = Life energy in the body: As long as you can, focus your attention on your body energy. Feel it in your body. Can you notice fine vibrations and tingling? This is your body energy.

When? How often? The formula is 3 x 3, which means that you practice BELL three times in a row and three times a day. In addition, you can use the technique at any time in between if you need some relaxation quickly. It is best to repeat the sequence three times.

Tips & Tricks

- **Tip**: the longer you exhale, the greater the relaxation effect.
- **Body Energy**: It is very relaxing when you focus your attention on your body energy. Stay with it as long as you can. With some training, you can stay with it for hours. You will find that it is very beneficial. This will detract attention away from your thoughts.

  Tip: You can also direct your attention to a point and feel your body energy there. I recommend the middle of your chest. That is where the heart chakra is. This is an important energy center. So just focus your attention on your heart chakra and try to feel the fine vibrations or a tingling sensation.

- **Body energy - a short exercise**: Close your eyes and take your attention inside the body. Focus your attention on your right hand. Do you feel a slight tingling or vibration? Take your attention through the whole body. You will feel these vibrations and the tingling everywhere. Eckhart Tolle calls this the inner body. You are welcome to listen to a guided meditation on YouTube: http://tinyurl.com/innererKoerper
- **Close your eyes**: If you can, close your eyes and feel your body.
- **The more, the better**: More than 3 breaths are

even better. You can also make it a kind of meditation and practice the technique for 10 to 15 minutes.

- Exhale with an aaahhhhh sigh. That feels good.
- **Effect on several levels**: Fears and stress are accompanied by flat, fast breathing and physical tension. In this technique, you consciously relax your muscles and breathe deeply and slowly. This automatically has a very relaxing effect. In addition, there is "smiling". This immediately lifts your mood. When you feel your body energy afterward, you draw off the energy from your negative thoughts. So, BELL works on several levels against tension.

Irena practices BELL about five times a day, each time practicing three times. "Six times a day is a lot, but I can feel the effect quite clearly. I am much more relaxed. Before practicing, I was restless, in a rush all the time even if I didn't need to. I even suffered from anxieties, mainly related to my job and my little daughter. She is so fragile and often ill. When unpleasant feelings come up or I get hectic, I immediately do BELL. That helps. In the beginning, I often didn't notice when I was getting hectic. That was normal for me. But over time I have become mindful of it and now more and more often I manage to break this habit with BELL."

Call to Action

Try BELL now. Practice the technique three times in a row. How do you feel after it? More relaxed, more serene?

Resources

BELL is presented for the first time in my German book *Joyful Mindfulness*. In this book, you will find a total of 50 habits for living happily in the here and now.

2.6 Energy techniques to quickly combat your anxiety

"Energy can therefore be regarded as the basic substance of our world." – Werner Heisenberg

What you can look forward to in this chapter:

- Fighting fears on an energy level
- The 4-Minute Chi Boost for a fast energy boost
- Eutaptics is the fast version of EFT

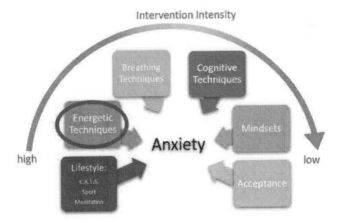

Since science has been able to prove that acupuncture

works, we definitely know that our body is traversed by energy pathways called meridians. Diseases are associated with disturbances in the energy system. Fear also causes a defect in the energy system. This means that if we eliminate the energy disorder, we heal the fear. Resourceful researchers have made use of this and found new ways of solving mental problems: This has birthed energy psychology.

In this book, I present two highly effective techniques:

- **4-Minute Chi Boost**: This is a technique that strengthens and heals the whole energy system of our body. It also improves our nervous system. This method is similar in effect to yoga, tai chi, and meditation. The advantage is that it is the turbo energy technique.
- **Eutaptics**: This is the latest development in energy psychology. You can use it to specifically treat psychological problems like, anxiety, depression, etc. But pain can also be healed with it. As the name suggests, the technique works quickly. And not only that, it is very easy to learn.

4-Minute Chi Boost[1]

The benefits of Qi Gong are nothing short of fantastic. According to recent studies, it has the same positive effects as meditation: for example, it reduces depression

[1] Lee, William. 5-Minute Chi Boost - Pressure Points for Reviving Life Energy, Avoiding Pain and Healing Fast.

symptoms and has a possible positive effect on diabetes.

In one study, researchers investigated Qi Gong's effect on cell aging. They looked at people with chronic fatigue syndrome: Those who had practiced Qi Gong for months showed significantly higher telomerase rises and improvements in their fatigue levels than those on a waiting list. Why is a rise in telomerase important? It signals self-rejuvenation: our biological clock is turned back. [1]

How can you harness the age-defying power of Qi Gong? Through the 4-Minute Chi Boost.

The 4-Minute Chi Boost is an exercise that combines four great Qi Gong techniques. It takes only four minutes to complete but its impact on the body and mind is immense and felt right away. Not only is the exercise immediately balancing and energy-boosting, but it also has the potential to heal diseases when practiced over a longer period.

The 4-minute Chi-Boost packs a whole bar of merits! That's according to Sifu Lee Williams, one of the leading experts in Qi Gong. It:

- Boosts energy

---

[1] Ho, R. T. H., et al., »A Randomized Controlled Trial of Qigong Exercise on Fatigue Symptoms, Functioning, and Telomerase Activity in Persons with Chronic Fatigue or Chronic Fatigue Syndrome«, Annals of Behavioral Medicine 44, No. 2 (October 2012): S. 160–170, doi:10.1007/s12160-012-9381-6.

- Alleviates stress and anxieties
- Eliminates headaches
- Enhances performance
- Promotes healing.

How can a 4-minute exercise alleviate anxiety? For one thing, it heals on all levels: As the body is strengthened on an energetic level, anxiety is automatically reduced. It also has elements that work directly against fears, like the kidney boost. According to Chinese medicine, fears are caused by a disturbance of the flow of kidney energy.

While the technique is designed for long-term practice, you'll experience these benefits starting right after your first session.

Let's now look at how to do it.

Action Plan

To do the 4-Minute Chi Boost, you will perform four individual techniques one after the other: I like to do it in the morning.

Goal: Energy boost, anxiety, and stress relief, healing

Basic Technique: It's important that you breathe in and out deeply into your stomach during the whole exercise. Always keep your tongue on the upper palate.

1. Energy Clapping (1 Minute 15 seconds)

This first exercise stimulates your energy and reduces stress. All the important meridians are addressed.

Clap your whole body with the palm of your hand. The energy clapping comes from Qi Gong. When you clap your hands, tap your body hard with the palm of your hand. It should be so strong that it almost hurts. Nevertheless, you should feel comfortable with it. Basically, you always start tapping on the left part of your body.

To see an illustration, watch the following video: https://www.youtube.com/watch?v=LQpy-peRCyQ. If you are in a hurry, watch it up to 1:40 minutes. That's quite enough, but it's worth watching the rest of it too.

2. Kidney Boost (1 Minute)

In Qi Gong, the kidneys have many important functions. In fact, anxiety is related to a malfunction of the kidneys.

Rub your palms together briskly for about 30 seconds so that they get really warm. Then place your hands flat on your kidneys and rub for about 45 seconds. Firmness and intensity should increase.

That's it. Your kidney energy is stimulated.

3. Double Power Tapping (45 seconds)

This has many positive effects, like improving the immune system, activating energy, and reducing stress.

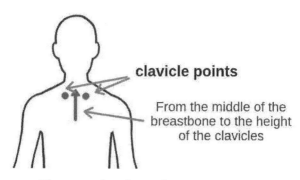

clavicle points

From the middle of the breastbone to the height of the clavicles

a. Thymus gland tapping

With your fingertips, tap yourself thirty times for *30 seconds* from the center of your chest to the height of your clavicles. This will stimulate the thymus gland.

b. Clavicle points

Tap the Clavicle points fifteen to twenty times for *15-20 seconds*. Where do you find them? Below the head of any clavicle. Find a soft, slightly pressure-sensitive spot—this is the collarbone point—and tap it hard with your fingertips. First the left, then the right. You can also tap both at the same time.

4. Ear massage (1 Minute)

Did you know that your ears are a reflection of your body? All organs, your brain, your spine, etc., can be found on your ears. In fact, traditional Chinese Medicine knows more than a hundred acupuncture points on each ear. This is why the ear massage not only has a relaxing effect but also activates your vitality, stimulates circulation, promotes concentration, stimulates self-healing, and has a positive effect on all organs and body parts. In one minute you'll have vitalized your whole body. That's what I call efficiency.

How you do it? Massage both your ears for about a minute, as explained below:

- Massage both ears at the same time. Start with the earlobes. Then knead and rub all ears, always as hard as possible. It works best with the thumb, index finger, and middle finger. Do not forget the cartilage.
- Finally, fold the ears together in the middle, then pull the earlobes down, and finally turn the ears forwards and backward.

That's it. You did well.

If you want to see how the ear massage works, I recommend the following video:
https://www.youtube.com/watch?v=uJveMkFshgo

How often and how long should you do the 4-Minute Chi Boost? One to ten rounds should do it, daily and whenever you want to reduce anxiety or need an energy boost. If you want to work on health impairments, you should do the 4-Minute Chi Boost for at least twenty-one days.

- **Anxiety and panic**: Use this routine in acute cases of stress and see for yourself how effective it is. You can also do it prophylactically. If you use it for a few weeks, your whole system will be strengthened so that anxiety or stress can no longer occur so easily.
- **Diseases**: You can also use this routine for

113

illnesses. Depending on the severity of the illness, you should do several rounds.

- **Energy Boost**: Do it whenever you need an energy boost. If one round is not enough, do several. You can't do anything wrong.

Tips, Tricks, & Reminders

- Remember to take a deep breath and leave your tongue on your upper palate. Throughout the routine, your breath should be even.
- Don't do it before going to bed: The technique gives you an energy boost, so do it at least two hours before bedtime.
- Do not do the 4-Minute Chi Boost:
  During pregnancy (eleven weeks or more) or lactation.
  In the case of open wounds or new injuries (shortly after an accident and when there is still swelling, inflammation, and/or fractures, or immediately after any type of surgery).
  If you have a pacemaker.

Besides these important exceptions, I wholeheartedly encourage you to start the **4-Minute Chi Boost right now**.

- **"But it seems complicated!"**: Trust me, it's easier than it looks. Once you've done the entire routine five times, it'll be effortless. You need some practice, but that's the case with almost all things.
- Here's a tip: Learn the routine in steps. Start with one part of the 4-Minute Chi Boost and add one more part to your routine every day, until you

114

master the entire exercise. Here's an example:

- **On Monday,** immediately after waking up, practice the energy clap (the first exercise of the 4-Minute Chi Boost).
- **Repeat this on Tuesday** morning and add the kidney boost.
- **On Wednesday,** repeat Tuesday's routine but add the double-tapping to the other two techniques.
- **Thursday:** To the energy clapping, kidney boost, and the double tapping, additionally practice the ear massage. You've now completed the entire routine.
- **Friday, Saturday, and Sunday:** For the rest of the week, practice the 4-Minute Chi Boost in full.

Done! You've mastered the 4-Minute Chi Boost.

It's (1) an easy way to reap the amazing healing and rejuvenating benefits of Qi Gong, (2) requires no special equipment, (3) is as good as meditation but only requires four minutes of your time, and (4) is easy to learn and something you can start right away, however busy you are. Why wait?

Resources

You can find a similar method in *5-Minute Chi Boost - Pressure Points for Reviving Life Energy, Avoiding Pain and Healing Fast*, by Lee William.

Eutaptics

Now I come to a technique from the field of energy

psychology. There are many different methods. The best-known method is EFT. Here certain acupressure points are stimulated. This means that acupressure is combined with techniques from NLP (Neurolinguistic Programming) and kinesiology. From personal experience, I can say that these kinds of tapping techniques work very well, especially with fears.

I can still very well remember how I came across this technique. I had a toothache. The day before, I had bought a little booklet about EFT (Emotional Freedom Technique), one of the first variations of these tapping techniques. Since I didn't want to take painkillers, I thought I'd just try it out. With the opened booklet in my left hand, I used this technique. I had to tap several points on my body and face with my fingers. It felt a bit strange, but I thought to myself: "The proof of the pudding is in the eating". To my astonishment, this technique worked! My toothache disappeared after a few minutes. However, I have to say that the pain was not particularly severe. Nevertheless, I was very impressed.

The tapping techniques were developed further. The newest and fastest variant is Eutaptics. This tapping technique uses fewer acupuncture points and has been simplified overall. Eutaptics was developed by Robert Smith and is a combination of NLP (neurolinguistic programming), hypnosis and energy psychology. It is very effective and quick to learn. It helps with all kinds of psychic diseases. Also, physical diseases can be treated with it. Eutaptics helps in the following cases:

- Weight loss, freedom from weight problems

- Allergies and eczema
- Anxiety and panic attacks
- Quitting smoking
- Depression
- Diabetes
- Skin diseases and psoriasis
- Migraine and headaches
- Dyslexia

In the following, a field report, from Danial, who had a very unusual fear:

Danial had a lot of anxieties about money. Here's his field report "Before I found Eutaptics, I had tremendous anxiety that affected every part of my life. I remember that when I received my paychecks, the anxiety was so intense that I spent it all in just a few days. At that time, I was not aware of the emotional state I was in. When I started using Eutaptics, everything changed: Today I am completely at peace with my life, have money and good friends. It's really amazing and the benefits and changes I've had with this method [Eutaptics] have gone beyond what I expected."

So much for the preface. Now let's start with the technique:

Action Plan

Goal: Reduction of negative feelings and thoughts, healing

Technique:

1. Aiming: Aiming is an important step. Ask yourself: "How do I know I'm scared? Is it an inner picture, noise or feeling?"

Notice how you know it and how you feel it in your body.

Example: Suppose you are worried about your work performance. Ask yourself: "How do I know that I'm worried?" You may have physical symptoms: Your heart beats a little faster or you have a lump in your belly. Or there are feelings like anger or irritation. At the same time, an inner image of your workplace emerges, how your boss criticizes you. This is the representation of your feelings. "The stronger you feel it, the faster it will go." Tell yourself that this is the last time you will feel it.

2. Assign the problem a number on the SUD scale (Subjective Units of Distress). This is a scale from 0 (= no load) to (10 = maximum load, e.g. panic). This assessment is completely subjective. You assign a four to the anxiety you have. Someone else would assign a 6 to the same fear. The main thing here is that you can follow the success of the technique.

3. Attunement for your subconscious: Here we go. Your subconscious is prepared for the healing process with an image: "Imagine we are taking away the roots of a tree. What would automatically happen? That's right, it would fall down and die."

Alternatively, you can use another image: "Imagine holding a bundle of helium balloons in your hand. What would automatically happen if you opened your fist?

Exactly, the balloons would fly away."

Choose one of the two images and use it before each healing session. Just imagine the image as vividly as possible.

4. Tap the meridian points and say: "Let it go, let it go, let it go ". You focus your attention on the individual meridian points.

It is best to tap the individual points about 10 times with your index and middle finger. You can tap quite strongly. It shouldn't hurt, but it should be noticeable. In the following picture, the meridian points are marked red.

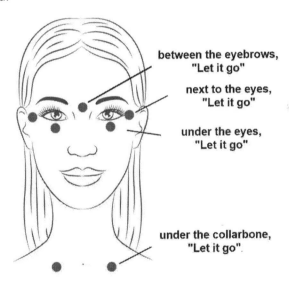

Source: Designed by Freepik

The individual meridian points are easy to find.

Between the eyebrows: This point is assigned to the bladder. It lies in the middle between the eyebrows.

Next to the eyes (gallbladder): These two points are on the bone next to the eyes.

Under the eyes (stomach): These two points are directly under the eyes, in the middle of the eye bone.

Collarbone point (kidney): Go from the hollow of the neck to a collarbone. It doesn't matter which one. In the beginning, there is a small hollow directly under the clavicle. Tap there. In Chinese teaching, the kidneys are linked to fear. So, when you are afraid, you often have an imbalance in kidney energy.

Tip: You only need to tap one side at a time - that's enough. So not both points next to your eyes, but only the right side or the left side. You can decide for yourself.

Say, "Peace"

Press wrist gently

Source: Designed by Yanalya / Freepik

5. Clasp your wrist and press it. Exhale deeply and say: "peace".

6. Now imagine a happy memory. Perhaps you imagine the last time you were in love. Imagine the situation so that you feel genuinely good. You can also remember your last holiday. The main thing is that you feel good about it.

7. Now check how you are with the help of the SUD scale. Repeat points 4 to 6 until you reach zero on the SUD scale.

How long? How often? Whenever anxiety arises, you can use this technique. You can also preventively reduce fears.

Tips & Tricks

- **Zero on the SUD scale**: Make sure you actually tap until the load drops to zero.
- **Start with less intense feelings**. It's advisable to gain confidence with this method first, before venturing to strong anxiety or panic. Start with worries or slighter anxieties. It will motivate you and give you security if you successfully break down these feelings.
- **Symptoms and images may change during treatment**. Then treat the new ones. Suppose you are afraid of flying. It manifests as an accelerated heartbeat. After a few rounds of Eutaptics, this symptom has disappeared, but you feel a slight pain in the kidney area. Then treat that.
- **Peace list**: You can make a list of all events and

topics that cause unpleasant feelings. You then work through this list day by day. This means that every evening you take a topic from the list and work on it with Eutaptics. So, step by step, you will experience more peace in your life.

Call to Action

Pick a slightly unpleasant emotion, like worry, restlessness, etc. Treat it with Eutaptics until it has a zero on the SUD. Celebrate your success!

Resources

There are many videos on Eutaptics on YouTube on all possible topics. Just type "Eutaptics" or "Faster EFT" into the search mask and you will see a lot of results. If you want to fight your fear with it, then search for "Eutaptics Anxiety". The inventor of Eutaptics, Robert G. Smith, has a highly recommended blog: https://Eutaptics.com/blog/. There are a lot of tips and reports.

2.7 (Not quite so...) short summary

- Mindset is the lens through which we see the world. People who have anxieties often have a negative mindset: "The world is uncertain and dangerous." Positive mindsets, on the contrary, are very helpful. They put you in a positive state, give you courage and open up resources.
- The Growth Mindset sees all the adversities of life as an opportunity to grow. Anxiety makes you a hero.

- With the mindset "The universe is friendly" a positive intention is assumed? behind everything.
- "Everything is transient" is the third mindset. It reminds us that life is valuable. At the same time, it makes it clear to us that even negative feelings like panic are short-lived.
- There are three alternatives to bringing mindsets into our lives: The exercise "Power Person", "Three Examples" and Affirmations. You can use these methods individually or simultaneously.
- Your lifestyle can contribute to anxiety.
- Sport reduces fears. 5000+ steps several times a week are enough to reduce your anxiety.
- Meditation is a particularly effective way to reduce anxiety.
- Food such as caffeine, alcohol, tobacco, and sugar or artificial sweeteners can cause anxiety.
- Anxiety is caused by negative thoughts. We can now interrupt the thoughts so that no anxieties arise in the first place or we can make the thoughts lose their effect.
- The Delete Key is the new generation of thought-stopping techniques. Not only does it stop thoughts, but it also triggers good feelings.
- The Sedona method has already helped hundreds of thousands of people. With the Sedona method, you can let go of fears.
- The Work questions whether thoughts are really true. Anxiety thoughts are always untrue. By seeing this, you take the power away from those thoughts.

- The Work Plus adds another important ingredient: affirmations. These are very effective in reducing anxiety.
- Breathing techniques interrupt the anxious breathing rhythm and therefore work powerfully against anxiety.
- You can use 4-7-8 breathing at any time. It is more effective against anxiety and panic than any medication.
- BELL contains the strongest physical counter-measures against anxiety: deep breathing, smiling and conscious relaxation of the body.
- Anti-panic breathing combines 4-7-8 breathing with energy methods and is therefore particularly effective.
- Anxiety is a disturbance of the physical energy system. Therefore, fear can be reduced by improving the flow of energy.
- The 4-Minute Chi Boost raises the overall energy level. As the name says, you need no more than five minutes. It is an excellent morning exercise.
- Eutaptics is the evolution of EFT. With this technique, fears, worries, and panic can be released quickly and purposefully.

Download your free audio meditation

You will get an audio meditation from me as a gift. Under this link you can download it for free and without any obligation:

https://detlefbeeker.de/body-scan/

Chapter 3: Three-week plans: simple, step-by-step instructions

"A calm sea does not make a good sailor."

What you can look forward to in this chapter…

- Three 3-week programs for worries, anxiety, and panic
- The five pillars you can defeat anxieties with

The programs you will get to know on the following pages are effective. They will help to alleviate your worries, fears, and panic. Your journey may not be over after three weeks, but you will feel much better.

The programs have been carefully put together. However, you are welcome to adapt it to your needs. If a technique works particularly well for you, feel free to use it more often than suggested in the program. For example, according to the plan, you should only practice the 4-Minute Chi Boost once a week. If it works for you, practice it daily! Why not? You can't use these techniques too often. But be careful not to overburden yourself.

There are two things you should avoid:

- Please do no less than the must-do program. You will read about what exactly this is at the beginning of the next chapter. Otherwise, it may not seem reasonable.
- Please don't stop earlier, you really want to keep

the program going for 3 weeks.

Remember: The most important ingredient is endurance. It is important that you consistently follow the program for three weeks. Commit yourself to maintain the three weeks. A few tips on how to commit yourself:

1. StickK.com: This page is about giving you an extra motivational boost to build your habits. For example, you want to start jogging daily tomorrow. You can deposit money at StickK.com. You lose your money if you don't jog every day. This can be very motivating. It should be an amount that hurts if you lose it. So not five euros, but rather 200 euros/ € 200. The StikK.com website is great. There are other ways to commit. Take a look at the site - it's worthwhile.

2. Motivation: You want to reduce fear. Why? If you are always aware of your reasons, this is a constant source of motivation. There are two types of motivation:

- **Negative motivation**: This is not a bad thing, by the way. It means that you want to avoid something. Maybe you want to prevent getting sick, losing your job or increasing fears. This can often be a strong impulse. Think about what negative reasons you have.
- **Positive motivation**: This means that you want to achieve something. So, do not reduce stress, but build mindfulness, become happier or healthier.

Your task now is to take a piece of paper and write down all the reasons you can think of without internal censorship. Of course, you can also do it in your notebook. It is important that you do it freely, without any inner censorship. Let it flow. It doesn't have to be ordered. Just write them down.

Now you may have written a whole page or even filled two. Now choose the five most important reasons. Of course, you can change the reasons later. If you have motivation problems now, you can become aware of these reasons. You can hang them up on your fridge, enter them into your mobile phone and have them displayed regularly, or you can recite them in the morning after getting up. You can also use them as an affirmation: This means that if you're not motivated right now, you'll see these five reasons.

3.1 Panic: The 3-Week Program

"Courage is when you're scared to death, but still get in the saddle." – John Wayne

Panic is an extreme feeling of fear. Panic lasts between five and 30 minutes. Because the feeling is so unpleasant, people want to avoid panic at all costs. There is a fear of panic. This means that if we want to fight panic effectively, we have to address two problem areas:

1. Panic: The first is acute panic itself.

- You can apply **Anti-Panic Breathing** (see the chapter "Three effective anti-panic switches"). They are very effective.

  Robert used to suffer from panic. It appeared

about once a week. He suffered from it a lot. I recommended that he use anti-panic breathing. He trained at it in quiet phases. When he came to me in our next session, his eyes were shining. He said, " The breathing works! The panic was gone within 20 seconds! I am so relieved".

The anti-panic breathing should be trained. During a panic attack, it is very difficult to do anything at all. The feelings and thoughts may overwhelm you. If the affected person manages to use the Anti-Panic Breathing for only three to 10 breaths, the panic is as good as gone. Nevertheless, it should be trained beforehand so that you can really use it in all cases.

- **The Work Plus and Eutaptics**: In addition, you should work preventively. You do this with The Work Plus (see chapter "Warning: Your thoughts may be dangerous") and Eutaptics (see chapter "Energy Techniques"). What does it look like? If you start to apply The Work Plus to your panic, fears may well arise. This is unpleasant and a reason why many people don't use The Work in the first place. This is where Eutaptics comes in. Every time anxiety occurs during The Work Plus, you do one, two or more rounds of Eutaptics. These two techniques complement each other perfectly. One works on your thoughts, the other energetically. So, you will quickly experience an improvement.

With The Work Plus, you work on what frightens

you about panic. On the other hand, you work on the reasons for panic.

- **Baby panic**: Panic is easiest to fight before it has fully developed. Panic doesn't fall from the sky. No, it develops. That means that if you feel signs of panic, that is, when the first baby panic occurs, you have to interrupt it. There are different techniques in this book. You can immediately use anti-panic breathing, which is always a good choice. Other techniques are The Delete Button (see chapter "Warning: Your thoughts may be dangerous"), Eutaptics or 4-7-8 breathing (see chapter "Three Effective Anti-Anxiety Switches").
- **Mindset:** A good mindset (see chapter "Powerful mindsets") is very supportive. Whether you see panic as a problem or a challenge makes a huge difference. Overcoming panic takes courage, motivation, and perseverance. Here, a positive mindset can be very important.

2. Fear of panic: All people affected are always afraid of panic. This is almost more problematic than the panic it-self. Why? Because it becomes a constant companion. Panic victims are constantly on the alert. A panic lasts only a few minutes, but the fear of panic is a constant companion. What can you do about it?

- **The Work Plus and Eutaptics**: You do The Work Plus and Eutaptics as described above.
- **Baby Anxiety**: The weaker the feeling, the easier it is to let it go. So, when your anxiety has only just occurred, it's still small, it's a baby anxiety. Here, you can use the delete key, Eutaptics or 4-7-

8 breathing. I recommend using the delete key in conjunction with affirmations you have gained from The Work Plus. That is, you first do the delete button and then you say your affirmations.

- **Cultivating Relaxation**: A person is constantly accompanied by anxiety and restlessness. That's why we should cultivate relaxation. That is, we try to create a relaxed state as often as possible. The best way to do this is meditation. Meditation is THE anti-anxiety remedy. Meditation will improve your whole life. In addition, you can incorporate small islands of relaxation into your everyday life. When you have some time, practice the BELL technique (see Chapter "Three effective anti-anxiety switches"). 30 seconds suffice in order to relax a little.

- **Lifestyle**: If you are stressed at work, only sleep for four hours, drink too much alcohol and consume ten cups of coffee a day, it is not surprising that you suffer from anxiety and panic. It's just too much. So, you should improve your whole lifestyle. Get enough sleep, don't drink too much, avoid coffee if possible, and exercise. There are many ways to increase your energy level. A great way is to start the day with the *4-Minute Chi Boost* (see chapter "Energy Techniques"). This gives you strength and vitality.

The fight against panic is therefore based on five pillars. The first three points are a must, points four and five are optional.

1. Master acute panic through **Anti-Panic Breathing**

(see chapter "Three effective anti-panic switches").

2. Prevention through **The Work Plus** (see chapter "Warning: Your thoughts may be dangerous") and **Eu-taptics** (see chapter "Energy Techniques").

3. **Mindset**: Choose one of the mindsets (see the chapters "Powerful Mindsets"): "Growth Mindset", "The universe is friendly" or "Everything is fleeting".

4. Cultivate relaxation through **meditation** (see chapter "Body Scan") and **BELL** (see chapter "Three Effective Anti-Anxiety Switches").

5. Improve lifestyle and strengthen the nervous system through sp**ort, meditation, C.A.T.S., and 4-Minute Chi Boost** (see chapter "Energy Techniques").

In the program, a distinction has been made between "must" and "can". On Monday it says under "must": Diary. This means that you should keep a diary. With "can" it says 5,000 steps. This is optional. If it suits you, you can take 5,000 steps, but you don't have to. The more can-do techniques you practice, the faster the program works. However: Don't overtax yourself. So, if you don't have much time, just do the must-do techniques. The minimum program consists of the must-do techniques, the maximum program of the must and can techniques.

"Case-by-case" means that these techniques are used when panic or anxiety occur. You can always use them.

First week

Case-by-case: *Anxiety*: Delete Button + affirmations;

panic: Anti-Panic Breathing

Monday: *Must*: in the morning, Power Person (see chapter "Powerful mindsets -> growth mindset"), diary. *Can*: 5,000 steps (see chapter "You must consider this forgotten factor... -> Sport")

Tuesday: *Must*: Journal, The Work Plus, and Eutaptics, 5 x anti-panic breathing. Do this breathing five times during the day, four breaths each. *Can*: five minutes of meditation, 5 x BELL

Wednesday: *Must*: Power Person (morning), Journal, The Work Plus, and Eutaptics, 5 x anti-panic breathing. *Can*: 5,000 steps, 5 x BELL

Thursday: *Must*: Journal, The Work Plus, and Eutaptics, 5 x anti-panic breathing. *Can*: five minutes of meditation, 5 x BELL

Friday: *Must*: Journal, The Work Plus, and Eutaptics, 5 x anti-panic breathing. *Can*: 5,000 steps, 5 x BELL

Saturday: *Must*: Journal, The Work Plus, and Eutaptics, 5 x anti-panic breathing. *Can*: 5 minutes of meditation, 5 x BELL

Sunday: *Must*: Power Person (morning). Can: 4-Minute Chi Boost

Tips & Tricks:

- **Case-by-case**: This means that whenever fears or panic arise, the appropriate techniques should be used. It is best if you catch the feelings in their baby phase.
- **Journal**: Keep a diary for one week. Identify

exactly when and under what circumstances fear or panic occurs. This is important! Use an app or notepad and write down exactly in which situation and at what time the feeling occurs. I know this is annoying. I ask you to do it anyway, even if only for a few days. Writing it down has some important advantages:

On the one hand, it can give *information about the causes*. Maybe your fears always appear after visiting the gym. This can indicate that you may be training too intensively and putting your body under too much stress.

On the other hand, you become *more mindful*. You now know the situations in which your negative feelings occur. This creates attention so that you do not react automatically. What do I mean by that? Negative feelings usually happen automatically. You get into a situation, negative thoughts automatically arise and the negative feeling appears. This process has become a habit. It happens over and over again. That's why you first have to create the awareness that you don't react automatically.

- **The Work Plus and Eutaptics**: Allow at least 15 minutes for this.
- **Meditation**: I strongly recommend meditation, but it is optional because I don't want to overwhelm you. Start with five minutes every other day.
- **Power-Person**: You can find this exercise in the

chapter "Powerful Mindsets". I recommend using it in the morning as it gives you a positive start to the day. You can also use one of the other mindset techniques instead if you prefer them.

- **Sports**: I have recommended 5,000 steps here. Of course, you can do other sports like jogging or cycling instead.
- **4-Minute Chi Boost**: Best in the morning. It makes a great start to the day.
- **Anti-Panic Breathing**: In the first week, you train it daily, so that you have it in case of panic.

Second week

Case-by-case: *Anxiety*: Delete Button + affirmations; *panic*: Anti-Panic Breathing

Monday: *Must:* Power Person (in the morning), The Work Plus and Eutaptics, consider when and in which situations your panic occurs. Has anything changed? *Can:* 6,000 steps, ten minutes of meditation, 5 x BELL

Tuesday: *Must:* The Work Plus and Eutaptics. *Can:* 6,000 Steps, ten minutes of meditation, 5 x BELL

Wednesday: *Must*: Power Person (morning), The Work Plus and Eutaptics, 5 x Anti-Panic Breathing *Can*: 6,000 Steps, 10 minutes of meditation, 5 x BELL, 4-Minute Chi Boost

Thursday: *Must*: The Work Plus and Eutaptics. *Can*: 6,000 Steps, ten minutes of meditation, 5 x BELL

Friday: *Must*: Power Person (morning), The Work Plus and Eutaptics. *Can*: 6,000 Steps, ten minutes of meditation, 5 x BELL

Saturday: *Must*: The Work Plus and Eutaptics, 5 x anti-panic breathing *Can*: 6,000 steps, ten minutes of meditation, 5 x BELL

Sunday: *Must*: Power Person (morning), *Can*: 4-Minute Chi Boost

Third week

Case-by-case: *Fear:* Delete Button + affirmations; *panic*: Anti-Panic Breathing

- **Monday:** *Must:* The Work Plus and Eutaptics. Think about when and in what situations your panic occurs. Has anything changed? *Can:* 7,000 steps, 15 minutes of meditation, 5 x BELL

Tuesday: *Must*: The Work Plus and Eutaptics. *Can*: 7,000 Steps, 15 minutes of meditation, 5 x BELL

Wednesday: *Must*: 5 x anti-panic breathing *Can*: 7,000 steps, 15 minutes of meditation, 5 x BELL, 4-Minute Chi Boost

Thursday: *Must*: The Work Plus and Eutaptics. *Can*: 7,000 Steps, 15 minutes of meditation, 5 x BELL

Friday: *Must*: The Work Plus and Eutaptics. *Can*: 7,000 Steps, 15 minutes of meditation, 5 x BELL

Saturday: *Must*: The Work Plus and Eutaptics. *Can*:

7,000 Steps, 15 minutes of meditation, 5 x BELL

Sunday: *Can*: 4-Minute Chi Boost

What's the next step?

You'll be feeling much more comfortable and relaxed now. The panic should no longer occur or, at least, it should have decreased considerably. There are several possibilities now:

- How much has your panic eased? Is it completely gone or do you now have worries instead of panic? Or do you still have fears, but they are not as intense anymore? Depending on your answer, you can continue with the following 3-week programs for fears or worries.
- You can also simply continue with the 3rd week (panic) program.
- You have now spent three weeks with all the techniques and have a good feeling as to which ones work best. Therefore, you can choose the techniques you liked best and create your own program.

All three possibilities are good and effective. Rely on your gut feeling. You can't do anything wrong.

3.2 Anxiety: The 3-Week Program

"A single principle will give you courage, namely that no suffering lasts forever." – Epikur von Samos

Fear emerges when we believe that something negative

will happen in the future. Fear is natural and even use-ful. It warns us about the dangers. Everyone is afraid now and again, that's normal. Even the Dalai Lama is afraid. It only becomes painful when anxiety becomes rampant. That is when it becomes irrational. Like an ir-rational fear of illness, even if there is no reason for it. Fear of losing one's partner, anxiety about losing one's job, etc. There are the most amazing fears, such as anat-idaephobia. This is the fear of being observed by a duck.

The five pillars with which we fight panic can also be ap-plied to anxiety. However, there are small differences.

1. Acute Anxiety: Here, I suggest the **Sedona method** (see chapter "Warning: Your thoughts may be danger-ous") or the **Delete Button** (see chapter "Warning: Your thoughts may be dangerous"). Both are great ways to stop thoughts and fears. Sedona goes a little deeper, but the Delete Button gives you good feelings.

2. Prophylaxis through The Work Plus (see chapter "Warning: Your thoughts may be dangerous") and Eu-taptics (see chapter "Energy Techniques"). Here, it de-pends on the intensity of the fear and how much you suffer from it. It may be sufficient if you only use the techniques recommended under Pillar 1.

I recommend that you use The Work Plus and Eutaptics anyway. This will help you get rid of your fears faster. That's why I've quoted The Work Plus and Eutaptics twice in the 3-week program.

3. Cultivate relaxation through meditation (see chapter "You must consider this forgotten factor...") and BELL (see chapter "3 effective anti-anxiety switches"). Anxiety affects the nervous system. We are restless and tense. Therefore, we should cultivate relaxation.

4. Improve your lifestyle through sport, meditation, C.A.T.S. and 4-Minute Chi Boost. The stronger we are, the less anxiety we have. Therefore, a healthy lifestyle and a high energy level are important.

5. Mindset: A good mindset is very supportive. Whether you see fear as a problem or a challenge makes a huge difference. Isn't it better if your fear is just a stone in your path of life instead of a huge problem?

As with the panic program, a distinction is made between can and must techniques. *Can* means that these techniques are optional. If you have enough time and motivation, do it. *Must* means that this technique is an integral part of the program. You have to do it.

On some days, such as Mondays, "must" means: "5 min. meditation or BELL or 5,000 steps". This means that you can choose one of the three techniques. Then stay with this technique for this week. So, if you choose "Meditation", you do "Meditation" this week on the corresponding days.

First week

Case-by-case: Delete Button or Sedona

Monday: *Must*: Power Person (see chapter "Powerful mindsets -> growth mindset") (morning), journal; 5 minutes of meditation or BELL or 5,000 steps (see chapter "You must consider this forgotten factor... ->

sports")

Tuesday: *Must*: Journal, The Work Plus, and Eutaptics. *Can*: 5 minutes of meditation, 5 x BELL

Wednesday: *Must*: Journal; 5 minutes of meditation or BELL or 5,000 steps

Thursday: *Must*: The Work Plus and Eutaptics. *Can*: 5 minutes of meditation, 5 x BELL

Friday: *Must*: 5 min meditation or BELL or 5,000 steps

Saturday: *Can*: 4-Minute Chi Boost

Sunday: *Must*: Power Person (morning). *Can*: 4-Minute Chi Boost

Tips & Tricks:

- **Case-by-case**: This means that whenever fears or panic arise, the appropriate techniques should be used. It is best if you catch the feelings in their baby phase.
- **Journal**: Keep a diary for one week. Identify exactly when and under what circumstances fear occurs. That's important! Use an app or notepad and write down exactly the situation and the time when the feeling occurs. I know this is annoying. I ask you to do it anyway, even if only for a few days. Writing it down has some important advantages:
On the one hand, it can provide **information about the causes**. Maybe your fears always appear after visiting the gym. This can indicate that you may be training too intensively and

putting your body under too much stress.

On the other hand, you become **more mindful**. You now know the situations in which your negative feelings occur. This creates attention so that you do not react automatically. What do I mean by that? Negative feelings usually happen automatically. You get into a situation, negative thoughts automatically rise and the negative feeling appears. This process has become a habit. It happens over and over again. That's why you first have to create the awareness that you don't react automatically.

- **The Work Plus and Eutaptics**: Allow at least 15 minutes for this.
- **Meditation**: I strongly recommend meditation, but it is optional because I don't want to overwhelm you. Start with five minutes every other day.
- **Power-Person**: You can find this exercise in the chapter "Mindset". I recommend using it in the morning because it gives you a positive start to the day. You can also use one of the other mindset techniques instead if you prefer them.
- **Sports**: I have recommended 5,000 steps here. Of course, you can do other sports like jogging or cycling instead.
- **4-Minute Chi Boost**: Do it best in the morning. That's a great start to the day. If you like it, do it more often. It strengthens your whole system.

Second week

Case-by-case: Delete Button or Sedona

Monday: *Must*: Power Person (morning), diary; 10 minutes of meditation or BELL or 6,000 steps

Tuesday: *Must*: Diary, The Work Plus, and Eutaptics. *Can*: 10 minutes of meditation, 5 x BELL

Wednesday: *Must*: Power Person (morning), journal; 10 minutes of meditation or BELL or 6,000 steps

Thursday: *Must*: "The Work Plus and Eutaptics. *Can*: 5 minutes of meditation, 5 x BELL

Friday: *Must*: 10 minutes of meditation or BELL or 6,000 steps.

Saturday: *Can*: 4-Minute Chi Boost

Sunday: *Must*: Power Person (morning), *Can*: 4-Minute Chi Boost

Third week

Case-by-case: Delete Button or Sedona

Monday: *Must*: Power Person (morning), diary; 15 minutes of meditation or BELL or 7,000 steps

Tuesday: *Must*: Diary, The Work Plus, and Eutaptics. *Can*: 15 minutes of meditation, 5 x BELL

Wednesday: *Must*: Power Person (morning), diary; 15 minutes of meditation or BELL or 7,000 steps

Thursday: *Must*: The Work Plus and Eutaptics. *Can*: 15 minutes of meditation, 5 x BELL

Friday: *Must*: 15 minutes of meditation or BELL or 7,000 steps

Saturday: *Must*: Power Person (morning), Can: 4-Minute Chi Boost

Sunday: *Can*: 4-Minute Chi Boost

What's the next step?

You'll be feeling much more comfortable and relaxed now. The anxiety should no longer be occurring or should at least have decreased considerably. There are several possibilities now:

- How much has your anxiety eased? Has it completely gone or do you now have worries instead? Depending on your answer, you can continue with the following 3-week programs for worries.
- You can also simply continue with the 3rd week (Anxiety-) program.
- You have now spent three weeks on all the techniques and have a good feeling as to which ones are working best. So, you can choose the techniques you liked best and create your own program.

All three possibilities are good and effective. Rely on your gut feeling. You can't do anything wrong.

3.3 Worries: The 3-Week Program

"99% of the things you worry about never happen."

Worries are less intense than fear, but they occur more frequently. They are the termites among the feelings: They are small but persistent. They gnaw and gnaw and gnaw until the tree falls. Since worries are not so painful, many people do nothing about them. They put up with them. That is completely ok, of course, but it is better to do something about them.

Basically, we can also use the pillars we have used for fear and panic when we are worried. It depends on how frequent your worries are. If worries occur here and there, it is quite enough to interrupt the worried thoughts. Here you can use the Sedona method or the Delete key. But if you are constantly worried, it can be useful to cultivate relaxation and raise your general energy level. Why? Because constant worry gnaws at your nerves. So, if we strengthen your nervous system, you'll have fewer worries. The following 3-week program is designed for frequent worries. As I said, if you are only worried occasionally, it suffices to interrupt your thoughts.

As with the panic program, a distinction is made between can and must techniques. Can means that these techniques are optional. If you have enough time and motivation, do it. *Must* means that this technique is an integral part of the program. You have to do it.

On some days, like Monday the program says "five minutes of meditation or BELL or 5,000 steps". This means that you can choose one of the three techniques. Then stay with this technique for this week. So, if you choose "Meditation", you do "Meditation" this week on the corresponding days.

First week

Case-by-case: Delete Button (see "Warning: Your thoughts may be dangerous" chapter) or Sedona (see "Warning: Your thoughts may be dangerous" chapter)

Monday: *Must*: Diary; 5 minutes of meditation (see chapter "You must consider this forgotten factor...") or BELL (see chapter "Three effective anti-anxiety switches") or 5,000 steps (see chapter "You must consider this forgotten factor... -> Sports")

Tuesday: *Must*: Diary. *Can*: 5 minutes of meditation, 5 x BELL

Wednesday: *Must*: Diary; 5 minutes of meditation or BELL or 5,000 steps

Thursday: *Must*: The Work Plus (see chapter "Warning: Your thoughts may be dangerous") and Eutaptics (see chapter "Energy Techniques"). *Can*: 5 minutes of meditation, 5 x BELL

Friday: *Must*: 5 minutes of meditation or BELL or 5,000 steps.

Saturday: *Can*: 4-Minute Chi Boost (see "Energy Techniques" chapter).

Sunday: *Must*: Power Person (see chapter "Powerful mindsets -> growth mindset") (morning), *Can*: 4-Minute Chi Boost

Tips & Tricks:

- **Case-by-case**: This means that whenever concerns arise, the appropriate techniques should be applied. It is best if you catch the feelings in their baby phase.
- **Diary**: Keep a diary for one week. Identify exactly when and under what circumstances worries occur. This is important! Use an app or notepad and write down exactly the situation and the time where the feeling occurs. I know this is annoying. I ask you to do it anyway, even if only for a few days. Writing it down has some important advantages:

  On the one hand, it can give you **information about the causes**. Maybe your worries always occur after a conversation with a colleague. This can indicate that you should avoid talking to this colleague because he or she always predict the worst catastrophes.

  On the other, you become **more mindful**. You now know the situations in which your negative feelings occur. This creates attention so that you do not react automatically. What do I mean by that? Negative feelings usually happen automatically. You get into a situation, negative thoughts automatically rise and the negative feeling appears. This process has become a habit. It happens over and over again. That's why you first have to create the awareness that you don't react automatically about not reacting automatically.
- **The Work Plus and Eutaptics**: Allow at least 15 minutes for this.

- **Meditation**: I strongly recommend meditation, but it is optional because I don't want to overwhelm you. Start with five minutes every other day.
- **Power-Person**: You can find this exercise in the chapter "Mindset". I recommend using it in the morning because it gives you a positive start to the day. You can also use one of the other mindset techniques instead if you prefer them.
- **Sports**: I have recommended 5,000 steps here. Of course, you can do other sports like jogging or cycling, instead.
- **4-Minute Chi Boost**: This is best in the morning. It's a great start to the day. If you like it, do it more often. It strengthens your whole system.

Second week

Case-by-case: Delete Button or Sedona

Monday: *Must*: Diary; 10 minutes of meditation or BELL or 6,000 steps

Tuesday: *Must*: Diary. *Can*: 10 minutes of meditation, 5 x BELL

Wednesday: *Must*: Diary; 10 minutes of meditation or BELL or 6,000 steps

Thursday: *Must*: The Work Plus and Eutaptics. *Can*: 5 minutes of meditation, 5 x BELL

Friday: *Must*: 10 minutes of meditation or BELL or 6,000 steps

Saturday: *Can*: 4-Minute Chi Boost

Sunday: *Must*: Power Person (morning). *Can*: 4-Minute Chi Boost

Third week

Case-by-case: Delete Button or Sedona

Monday: *Must*: Diary; 15 minutes of meditation or BELL or 7000 steps

Tuesday: *Must*: Diary, The Work Plus, and Eutaptics. *Can*: 15 minutes of meditation, 5 x BELL

Wednesday: *Must*: Diary; 15 minutes of meditation or BELL or 7,000 steps

Thursday: *Must*: The Work Plus and Eutaptics. *Can*: 15 minutes of meditation, 5 x BELL

Friday: *Must*: 15 minutes of meditation or BELL or 7,000 steps

Saturday: *Can*: 4-Minute Chi Boost.

Sunday: *Must*: Power Person (morning). *Can*: 4-Minute Chi Boost

What's the next step?

You'll be feeling much more comfortable and relaxed now. Your worries should no longer be occurring or should at least have decreased considerably. There are several possibilities now:

- You can also simply continue with the Week 3 program (Worries).

- You have now spent three weeks on all the techniques and have a good feeling as to which ones work best. Therefore, you can choose the techniques you liked best and create your own program.

All two possibilities are good and effective. Rely on your gut feeling. You can't do anything wrong.

3.4 In a nutshell

- There is a 3-week program for worries, fear, and panic. I recommend that you use it as it is.
- "Must" means that you should use these techniques in any case. "Can" means that if you have enough time and motivation, you should practice these methods. If possible, apply *must* and *can*.
- You will see that after three weeks a lot has already happened. Your fears will have decreased considerably.
- The goal of all techniques is to finally let go of all techniques. Techniques are like crutches: they are helpful during the healing process. When you are healed, you don't need them anymore.

Download your free audio meditation

You will get an audio meditation from me as a gift. Under this link you can download it for free and without any obligation:

https://detlefbeeker.de/body-scan/

Chapter 4: Bonus:
The Best Herbal Remedies for Anxiety

"Dear God! Can you make the vitamins from the spinach go into the custard?" – Anonymous

What you can look forward to in this chapter:

- The best herbal remedies for anxiety

So far, we have got to know a lot of techniques and suitable programs. You can support these techniques with herbal remedies. They are the gentle twin of allopathic medicines. Herbal remedies can be very effective against anxiety, but they have practically no side effects. Therefore, they are to be recommended in each case, since also the risk of becoming hooked on them is negligible. Let me introduce you to the best. They have an anti-anxiety effect, but also lighten and calm the mood.

Ginseng

There are a number of studies on the effects of ginseng. Proven effects include performance enhancement, anti-depressant, nerve-strengthening, improvement of the immune system and potency, and positive effect on the liver. Ginseng also has a regulating effect on blood sugar levels and blood lipids. Ginseng is slightly stimulating.

St. John's Wort

This plant is the best-studied herbal remedy. It has a mood-lifting effect and thus works against mild-to-moderate depression. The usual dosage is 300 milligrams, three times daily. However, the herb works slowly. The full effect can only be felt after two months of continuous use.

Roseroot (Rhodiola)

If you have mild to moderate depression or feel lacking in energy, you can take roseroot. Studies have confirmed that roseroot has a significant anti-depressive effect in mild and moderate depression. Dr. Weil, one of the leading experts in happiness research, recommends that you take 100 milligrams twice a day, in the morning and early afternoon. Taken too late, it can cause sleep problems. You can increase the dosage to 200 milligrams, three times daily, but again, be careful not to take it too late. Negative effects with other drugs have hardly been investigated, so you should ask your doctor here.

Ashwagandha

Studies have shown that Ashwagandha alleviates fears and has a mood-lifting effect. Dr. Low Dog, one of the leading experts in the field of herbal medicine, recommends taking 300-500 milligrams of this plant, two to three times a day. It has no sedating effect and can be taken during the day. According to Dr. Low Dog, Ashwagandha is one of the most effective herbal remedies for chronic stress, sleep problems, and lack of energy.

Valerian

This healing root has a long and successful history. It has a sleep-inducing and anti-anxiety effect. There is no danger of addiction. Use standardized valerian extract with 0.8% valerian acid. Take 250 milligrams with meals up to three times daily.

Kava

Kava works very well against anxiety. Studies have shown that kava works just as well against anxiety as benzodiazepines. There are rare reports that there are side effects on the liver. That's why people with liver damage should avoid this plant. Alcohol or antidepressants can be addictive. Otherwise, the root is safe. Dr. Weil recommends kava extract standardized to 30% kavapyrone. You take this up to three times daily in a dosage of 100 or 200 milligrams. It works quickly against anxiety. Do not take it for more than a few months.

4.1 In a Nutshell

- Valerian and kava work well against fears.
- Ginseng, rosewort, and St. John's wort are natural antidepressants.
- Ashwagandha has a mood-enhancing and anxiety-killing effect.

Chapter 5: Summary

"Not because it's hard, we don't dare, but because we don't dare, it's hard." – Aurelius

- Anxieties arise from the idea that something bad will happen in the future. Our thoughts are the main cause of fears. Fears are also influenced by the state of our nervous and energy systems.

- In the chapter "Techniques" I have collected the best techniques against fears. It includes mindsets, lifestyle, cognitive and energetic techniques.
- The goal is that the anxieties either dissolve completely or that you can accept them. Acceptance means that you allow the particular feeling or thought to be there. You have no resistance, but you give it space. This is not always easy, but the more you can accept, the more peace you will have.
- You support these techniques with a good mindset. How we perceive the world is determined by our mindset. It is the glasses through which we look at our universe. A positive mindset will help you greatly to fight your anxieties. In this book, you will find three mindsets that have worked very well: Growth Mindset, The universe is friendly, Everything is fleeting.
- Make sure that you do not promote your anxieties by an unfavorable lifestyle. Get enough sleep, exercise and meditate regularly. You should also pay attention to your intake of C.A.T.S.
- In case of strong anxiety and panic, you should combine Eutaptics with The Work Plus as a prophylaxis/preventative measure. In acute cases, use Anti-Panic Breathing, Sedona or the Delete Button.
- Energy psychology is quite a new branch of

psychology. According to energy psychology, anxiety is caused by disturbances in the energy system. Thus, we can heal fears through energy work. There are now a lot of studies that confirm effectiveness. I have introduced you to the 4-Minute Chi Boost. It increases and heals your energy system in general. You can also use it for physical illnesses. You got to know EFT. With this method, you can alleviate fears in a targeted way. It also works well with pain.

- There is a 3-week program for worries, fears, and panic. It compiles the techniques in such a way that fears are optimally combated. There are always some must-have techniques that you should practice in any case. There are also optional techniques that you should use if you have enough motivation and time. This means that you can adapt the programs to your specific situation.

- It is important that you actually stick with the three weeks. Please don't stop before. At least hold on to the must-do techniques for three weeks. You will see that the anxieties have already substantially eased afterward.

- After the three weeks, you can simply continue with the Week 3 program until your fears have completely disappeared or until you can accept them.

- Courage and persistence are the keys to success.

You belong to the extraordinary 3.2%

"Not the beginning is rewarded, but only the perseverance."

Do you hear the applause? This is from the author! You deserve it. Why? Because only 10% of readers go beyond the first chapter of a book, and you've even read the whole book! So, you see things through to the end - an important skill! Also, you are among the special group of readers who read self-help books. Only 32% of readers do this. By the way, we have something in common. I love self-help books too! Together, we belong to the chosen 3.2%. Well, that's worth the applause!

I put a lot of passion in this book. That's why I'm glad that you found it so interesting to read until the end. It gives me the courage to ask you for a small favor. It costs you nothing, but it would help me enormously: Would you take a minute or two to write a quick review? Two or three short sentences are enough. You can write them on the book page.

Maybe it seems unimportant, but every single review counts. Your positive review will help me continue to work as an independent author and write more books to help people.

Thank you so much!

Warm regards,

Detlef Beeker

Website of the author: http://detlefbeeker.de/en/

PS: If you do not like the book, please let me know. Any kind of feedback is valuable to me. Just write me an email to <u>detlef@detlefbeeker.de</u>.

Made in the USA
Middletown, DE
15 June 2020

98107107R00094